KARATE MASTER

KARATE MASTER

The Life and Times of **Mitsusuke Harada**

Dr.Clive Layton

Bushido Publications

Karate Master — The Life and Times of Mitsusuke Harada

First Published in 1997
by Bushido Publications,
P.O. Box 15, Liverpool, Merseyside L19 7PE, England.
Tel: 0151-494 1176. Fax: 0151-494 1192

Copyright © 1997 Clive Layton

Phototypeset by Bushido Publications

Printed by Page Bros, Norwich, Norfolk

British Library Cataloguing-in-Publication Data.
A catalogue record of this book is available from the British Library

Hardbound Edition ISBN 1 871457 01 7
Paperbound Edition ISBN 1 871457 02 5

To Rachel, Pandora and Cedar

BY THE SAME AUTHOR

Conversations With Karate Masters
Unmasking The Martial Artist
Mysteries Of The Martial Arts
Mind Training For The Martial Arts
Training With Funakoshi
Shotokan Dawn

Disclaimer

Neither the Author nor Publisher of this book will be held responsible in any way for injury or damage of any nature which may occur to readers, or others as a direct or indirect result of the information/instructions contained herein.

It is strongly recommended that the reader consult and seek the advice of a physician before attempting to follow any of the exercises/activities described, or depicted in this book. Karate training methods are by nature very specific and could well result in injury if this advice is not heeded.

The Publisher strongly advocates that people engaging in any Martial Arts study should exercise caution in training and also use discretion in application of their skills and knowledge.

Contents

Acknowledgments

The author and publisher are grateful to the following people for their considerable help during the preparation of this book:

Professor Bernard Mathieu, 5th *Dan*

Marie Kellett, 5th *Dan*

Stephen Hope, 5th *Dan*

Tony Lima, 5th *Dan*

Zygmunt Boban, 5th *Dan*

William Haggerty, 5th *Dan*

Roy Margetts, 4th *Dan*

Jon Lawrence, 4th *Dan*

Frank Riley, 3rd *Dan*

Ken Waight, 1st *Dan* (1966)
    (G.B. Head Instructor of *Shintaido* and *Kitaido*)

Joy Macquire

Rachel Layton

James Taylor (Imperial War Museum)

Graham Jones

Tracey Hepworth

Graham Noble

Steve Donovan

Gary McNamara

Preface

It is said that the gods move in strange and mysterious ways. What woke me was not the dawn light beaming in through the rippling curtains, nor the soft breeze that had picked up during the night and now entered through the barely opened window of my spacious 1930s hotel room. No, there was a presence in that room, something not felt when I had settled down the night before. It was watching me, I could sense the intensity of its glare. My bleary eyes began to focus. There…over there, on the back of the armchair, motionless, its shape barely visible in the shadowy half-light, perched a wild grey dove. It had entered the room most skilfully, squeezed through the gap in the window, swung under the lace curtains, and fearlessly negotiated the heavy cotton curtaining that hung down well below the window sill. This bird had a purpose. When the dove knew it had been seen, no attempt was made to escape. It just stared at me. And then, ever so softly, ever so gently, it began to coo its message — or so it seemed. Then it was gone.

The responsibility of what I was about to undertake that first morning and the months to follow suddenly and, one might say, inexplicably, came over me in a wave. I sat up, my mind too full of encounter and association to resume my slumbers. I had been entrusted to write a man's life story. The impression I gave might well be how he was to be remembered for all time. Each sentence had to be faithful. Believe me when I say that the spirit of Hermes was in that coo and in that dove, a messenger to man. Nature subsequently focused on my work, softened my intent, and gave me a different perspective on how it should all be presented. The searching had come to an end. If the author believed in such things he might well say, in a classic vein, that all was well and as it should be.

This book is about one rather special man's dedication to the art of Karate-Do. Mitsusuke Harada has travelled the Way of the 'empty-hand' for more than fifty years now, having never wavered from his path, but single-mindedly pursued, and built upon, that which his teachers gave him. And what teachers they were! Beginning training at the famous Shotokan, he was taught by the powerful Motonobu Hironishi, the elegant Wado

Uemura, and the disciplined Yoshiaki Hayashi. Harada knew the dynamic and spiritually-advanced Yoshitaka Funakoshi, who died young, yet whose influence is still so strong today. After the war, Harada had the enviable privilege of practising, as a private student, under Gichin Funakoshi, the Okinawan master credited with introducing Karate-Do to Japan, and the inspiration for what became known as the Shotokan and Shotokai styles. At university he trained under the exceptionally-gifted, but eccentric, Master Tadao Okuyama, an inspiration, whose questions still haunt him, and was a private student of Master Shigeru Egami, during the master's most enquiring and intense period. He assisted Hiroshi Noguchi of Waseda University, whose training was so severe, in teaching Karate to undergraduates, and Masatoshi Nakayama, Chief Instructor to the Japan Karate Association, on an influential course to American Airforce personnel. He was also a great friend and training partner to the legendary Tsutomu Ohshima, and practised with such world-famous Karate-ka as Taiji Kase and Hidetaka Nishiyama in the late Forties and early Fifties. There can truly be few men alive today who can claim such an exceptional training background.

With the influence of such teachers and contemporaries running through his veins, Master Harada introduced Karate-do to South America in 1955 with Gichin Funakoshi's personal blessing. He later taught briefly in France and Belgium before becoming the first Japanese Karate teacher to reside in Great Britain in 1963. He has subsequently positively influenced two generations of enquiring students, and now heads the small and friendly Karate-Do Shotokai (KDS) Association in Great Britain and the Karate-Do Shotokai France, and travels widely throughout Europe, Scandinavia and North Africa.

An intelligent and noticeably courteous man of quiet and reserved disposition, Master Harada has never sought the limelight, and consequently is not as widely known as he deserves to be. The author has heard many a famous Japanese and occidental master from varying martial arts speak of him with great respect. His style, in many ways so different from mainstream Karate practice, and the way of thinking, are advanced and often difficult for the experienced, let alone inexperienced, to comprehend and appreciate. He is, if such a thing were desirable, a master's master — the epitome of what

Karate-do can produce. To let his story go untold would be tantamount to a crime. Putting it plainly, without it the history of Karate-do would be incomplete.

Every serious Karate-ka, regardless of style — no, every martial artist, regardless of art, should, I feel, spend some time alone with Master Harada. Each, I am sure, would benefit greatly and the impression left would, no doubt, be a lasting one. This is clearly not possible, of course: Master Harada is now 65 years of age, and the devil is in the clock.

Both the author and the publisher, are extremely grateful to Master Harada for his time, co-operation and careful consideration, with regard to the production of this work. The author likes to think that all three share a common goal. You see, the Way of Karate has much to offer human beings, and yet it is so often conveniently misinterpreted, compromised, abused. Mitsusuke Harada has stayed true to the Karate ideal, despite personal hardship. Typically generous by nature, he has been prepared to share this hard-earned knowledge so that all may benefit. This then is his story.

Clive Layton, M.A., Ph.D.

December 1993.

1

A Student
At The
Shotokan

Yutaka Harada and his two sisters in Tokyo — circa 1917.

Toyotaro Harada had a sizeable lowland rice farm near Aomori in northern Honshu, by the Tsugaru Strait. Because of poor drainage, low winter temperatures and much snow, one, albeit substantial crop, was produced annually. Additional valuable revenue came as a result of harvesting apples and the felling of timber in the surrounding hills. Toyotaro's only son, Yutaka, was intent on another career, however. Born in 1896, Yutaka had, after much effort and a little encouragement, passed the examinations to the Second Public High School in Sendai, enabling him to study to become a doctor at Tokyo's Imperial University. But his father, under the influence of his son-in-law, was not willing to finance this education, for his son was expected to follow tradition and work the land. Having planned to come back home and set up a medical practice, Yutaka became deeply disillusioned and depressed by his father's action, and said that real ambition and zest for life discontinued from that point on. He never really forgave Toyotaro, and thereafter did his best to avoid the family home, his mother and two sisters.

Yutaka, a handsome, powerfully-built young man, standing over six feet in height, intent on avoiding the life of a farmer, joined the Japanese Army in 1914 for three years. Very quiet, bright and conscientious by nature, he soon passed the examinations for corporal and then sergeant, before taking a commission as a second lieutenant. He then entered Waseda University in 1917 and read for a bachelor's degree in commerce, before working in a Tokyo bank. Yutaka's education at Waseda was, in fact, paid for by his father, who by this time had succumbed to reason, but it was too late now for his son to become a doctor. In the mid-Twenties, to escape his family obligations, Yutaka moved to southern Manchuria, working in an administrative capacity for the South Manchurian Railway, with his new bride, Haru.

Born in 1897, into the Kuroda samurai family, Haru's ancestors had, from the mid-seventeenth century, served the formidable Lords Ikeda, whose family title was promoted to Marquis after the Meiji Restoration of 1868. The Kuroda ancestral home, where Haru was born, was at the castle town of Okayama, in Bizen Province, a little west of Kobe on southern Honshu. Before meeting her husband, Haru was a top journalist with the 'Mainichi Shimbun' (newspaper) in Osaka. At the time of writing she is aged 97, but confined to her bed, in Tokyo.

Yutaka and Haru's first child, Mitsusuke, was born on the

Mitsusuke Harada, aged three months.

16th November 1928, in the large seaport of Dairen, on the southern tip of Manchuria (now in Liaoning Province, China), overlooking Korea Bay to the east and the Yellow Sea to the south-east, some two hundred miles south of the then capital Mukden (now Shen-yang). The most densely-populated section of the country, the Liaotung Peninsula provided the Japanese with two ports free from ice in a country of extremes of climate — hot, windless summers and bitter winters with north winds. Elsewhere, the rivers of Manchuria were frozen for six months of the year. Picture these ports, if you will, Dairen and Port Arthur, on the east coast of a plain with two ridges of old, eroded mountains rising to fifteen hundred feet, to the north. Coal, iron, magnesium and oil shale were major mineral resources of the region, and the South Manchurian Railway had a great rivalry with the Chinese Railway, especially in the transport of the huge crops of wheat, millet, maize, rice, and in particular soya-beans. At one point considerable friction arose between Hulutao, a then recently much developed Chinese ice-free port on the Gulf of Liaotung, and Dairen.

Owing to the influx, not to say permanent migration, of a large number of Chinese peasants into southern Manchuria, and some alleged destruction of the South Manchurian Railway lines near Mukden, the Japanese entered Manchuria in September, 1931. The Imperial Army drove Marshal Chang Hsiao-Liang back to China, and set up the 'independent' nation or state of Manchuku in 1932. This naturally gave rise to much concern, and Yutaka entered the army reserve, protecting Japanese residents in this strategically important and troubled land.

Still fresh in Master Harada's mind, despite the passing of 60 years, was the occasion on which he was lined up, with all the other school children, flags in hand, to welcome the last descendant of the Manchu emperors of China. Harada, laughing, recalled that there had been much preparation to welcome Pu Li, the Last Emperor, and they had waited a long time by the road. The black limousine whisked past the crowds, and the welcome was over in an instant. Master Harada thought the whole episode a complete waste of time, and a considerable anti-climax for a child. Pu Li acted as a puppet head of the Manchuku state under the title of K'ang Te, with his residence at Ch'ang-ch'un (re-named Hsin-Ching). Enthroned as Emperor in 1934, he ended his days as a gardener in Mao's People's Republic.

Yutaka Harada in Manchuria with his favourite horse.

Whilst in Manchuria, Yutaka pursued his love of riding, was a member of the riding club, and kept two of their finest horses. He was a highly-competent horseman, particularly in the field of horse-jumping, and was a candidate for the 1928 Olympic Games held in Amsterdam. He had the distinction of being beaten in the selection procedure by a cavalry officer who, Harada believes, went on to win the gold medal. Yutaka had an affinity with these creatures, and as a child on the family farm, slept in the stable with his horse beside him. Master Harada remembers that his father used to give one particular thorough-bred a large carrot every day. On one occasion, due to work

Mitsusuke Harada (left) and his sister, Sadako, at infant school.

commitments, Yutaka asked his son to run down to the market to collect the carrots and give this horse his usual treat — but Mitsusuke forgot. After his father returned from his usual Saturday ride, he rebuked his son for not doing as he was asked. Yutaka knew that the temperamental thoroughbred had not received the carrot by the ride it gave. The highly-strung creature would sometimes bite his father, but he never retaliated, choosing to ride the horse for many hours at a time to show him just who was in command.

The young Mitsusuke was much impressed with his father's oneness with animals, and indeed Yutaka's care and respect for his fellow-man. In fact, Yutaka was a great sports and outdoors man all round, being very keen on tennis, baseball and fishing. At five o'clock in the morning, the two of them would rise and fish local rivers and lakes for carp, using sweet potato as bait. Fishing until mid-day, they often had catches of a respectable size. It was at times like this, or especially when his father returned home from a hard day at the office, that the two of them would go into the garden after dinner, and his father would tell stories of mysteries and far-away places. Harada remembers well that Yutaka would often talk of the sophistication of the Paris water and underground systems, and that these early conversations may have been, in part, the inspiration that created the urge to travel later in the master's life.

Yutaka's work involved the Harada family, which included Mitsusuke's younger sister, Sadako (who became a hat designer), living for a short while first in the great walled city of Peking (which had just lost its title of capital of China to Nanking), and then for a year in China's chief port situated on the Hwang-po, Shanghai. As Shanghai was the commercial and industrial centre of the region, the Japanese had bombarded the Chinese quarter of the city in 1932, and there was still a fair degree of hostility and mistrust when the Harada family arrived. But in 1938 Harada, along with his mother and sister, undertook a three-day boat trip to Japan, and moved to Tokyo for safety, his father staying in Manchuria.

Strange and surprising as it may seem, Master Harada said that his mother had been *"selfish"* and *"didn't really take care of us"* before and during the war years, preferring to socialise. He felt that he wasn't properly fed, was neglected, and now strongly resents missing out on a proper childhood. As an example of his mother's considerable insensitivity, Harada explained that when he was young his mother would tether him by his leg to a table, and then go out and leave him alone in the house! He explained that he could have easily been a wild young man if he had been unfortunate enough to have got in with the wrong company. It should be noted here that, because Mitsusuke and Sadako have never married or had children, both their mother's line (she was the only child) and the Harada line (through the male) will cease. In fact, the Harada name will continue through the female side, because one of Yutaka's sisters stayed on the farm, married and had children, her husband taking the Harada family name (which is quite acceptable in Japan).

Mitsusuke aged twelve years.

Just before the end of the Second World War, and following the Soviet Union's invasion of Manchuria, all Japanese property was confiscated and Yutaka was repatriated to Tokyo penniless, without a position and aged 49. The family home became a small property and with the exception of a few minor temporary accountancy jobs, Yutaka was never to work again. Fortunately, he had the foresight to invest in property in Japan whilst working in Manchuria, and he sold this off, little by little, through the subsequent years, which provided some additional income. His last years were happy ones spent at home with his wife and daughter, living on the rent they obtained from a number of

The inauguration of the Shotokan — the first purpose-built Karate dojo in Japan — on 29th July, 1939.

small apartments they owned in Tokyo. He enjoyed gardening and walking. He died in 1976 with no regrets. He never really spoke about his family though, and Harada acquired the above information after his father's death, from a monk who had known the family's history well.

Whilst in Manchuria the young Mitsusuke had seen some Chinese (employees of his father) practising the martial art of Tai Chi Chuan, but he couldn't speak Chinese and they couldn't speak Japanese, so his enthusiasm was frustrated. He was sufficiently impressed, however, to ask his father to look out for a *dojo* (training hall — though literally, 'place of the Way') for him the next time he went to Tokyo on business. This his father was pleased to do, and he headed for the Waseda Karate club, where he was given the address of the famous Shotokan. Mitsusuke had also been fortunate enough at one time to have lived opposite

**Master Gichin Funakoshi is seated between the centre banner and the
right side banner (far left of this page).**

Shigeyoshi Takano, a very famous Kendo man, who had won the
Japanese National Championships a number of times, and who
annually led a strong team from Manchuria. Harada did in fact
practise Kendo at his Middle School, which was customary, but
only for one year.

One evening in early November 1943, after a full day at the
Seigakuin Middle School, the excited and expectant 14-year-old
Harada visited the Shotokan and undertook his first Karate lesson. The reason for his early enthusiasm was simple — he
wanted to be strong, and was attracted to the novelty and power
of this relatively new martial art. The Shotokan was situated in
Zoshigaya, Toshima Ward, in a rather out-of-the-way location,
and was the first purpose-built Karate dojo in Japan, having been
erected in the spring of 1936 following private donations organised by one of Gichin Funakoshi's top students, Kichinosuke

Saigo, who later became a politician of note. The inauguration of the dojo was held on the 29th July 1939.

Over the entrance to the building, under a porch lamp, hung the name painted in bold white characters, chosen by the building committee, which when translated, read the 'Hall of Shoto'. Master Funakoshi signed his poems with the pseudonym '*Shoto*', the literal translation of which is: 'Pine waves'. The name came about as a result of nature's bewitching influence upon the master, especially after training, in his days in Shuri and Naha, on the island of Okinawa. Master Funakoshi, who lived next to the dojo (to the left as you entered the Shotokan grounds) instructed during the morning session each day he was there, and taught *kata* (forms — series of movements in set sequences regarded as the soul of Karate-Do). The old Okinawan master, who is credited with introducing Karate to Japan, was 75 years of age at the time, and had been in Japan 21 years when Harada started to train at the dojo.

December 1943 saw the master's fourth book, '*Karate-Do Nyumon*', an introduction to Karate-Do, come into print. (This book came in the wake of '*Ryukyu Kempo: Tode*' [1922], '*Rentan Goshin Karate-Tode*' [1925], and his most influential work,

Master Gichin Funakoshi leads a class in kata ('formal exercises') at Keio University, Tokyo — circa 1930.

Gichin Funakoshi of Okinawa: the former schoolteacher who is universally credited with introducing the art of Karate-Do to Japan. The Master is pictured here in his late eighties.

'*Karate-Do Kyohan*' [1935].) However this was at a stage in World War Two when paper was in short supply and the book was printed in very small numbers. So much so, in fact, that even Harada, training at the Shotokan, could not obtain a copy, though it was reprinted four or five years later. Master Harada did recall reading an article during this period that appeared in '*Shinbudo*' magazine, which bore Gichin Funakoshi's name. Harada believed that Gichin's son, Yoshitaka, actually wrote the piece.

A primary school teacher and later headmaster of 30 years, it was Funakoshi's mission in later life to spread the tradition and philosophy of Karate-Do so that all could benefit from the art. Before the war he had been given the award of *Renshi* by the Dai Nippon Butokukai, or, Great Japan Martial Virtues Association (founded in 1895). *Renshi* may be best described as the first level of master, awarded at the time at 4th *Dan* (degree) and later at 5th *Dan*, for technical excellence. There is, however, a story (which may well be true) that Master Funakoshi refused the award. One of his students, Yasuhiro Konishi, was on the panel that awarded Funakoshi the title, yet Konishi held the higher award of *Kyoshi*! I can still hear Harada laughing at this ridiculous situation. *Kyoshi* is the second level of master, nowadays normally awarded at 7th *Dan*, though sometimes at 6th *Dan*. It reflects great ability as a teacher. Chojun Miyagi, the founder of Goju-*Ryu* (martial tradition or system) Karate, was awarded *Kyoshi*. The highest level of master is *Hanshi*, where not only evidence of higher order technique and teaching are required, but excellent character. This award is not normally made below 8th *Dan* and some 40 years of practice.

Master Harada can remember his first lesson at the Shotokan very clearly, despite the lapse of more than 50 years. His instructor was the very powerful and formidable Master Motonobu (Genshin) Hironishi, who had been a sergeant in the Sino-Japanese war. There is an anecdote that Harada tells concerning an incident which supposedly occurred during Hironishi's time in the army. Hironishi was asked by an officer whether Karate was strong. The master's reply was to break a wooden gun-rack with his fist, much to the horror and dismay of those present. It is said that people tended to leave him alone and not ask inane questions after that! Hironishi had been born in a small fishing village and was always seeking ways to develop greater Karate

The powerful and formidable Motonobu (Genshin) Hironishi was always seeking ways to develop greater Karate strength. In these photos Master Hironishi is shown confronting the makiwara (striking post) and practising kicks wearing iron geta (clogs).

strength. He could apparently walk on his bent toes, and practised hard with heavy iron *geta* (clogs) and fist weights. Hironishi was, reputedly, Master Funakoshi's favourite student, though the no-less-talented Wado Uemura, who was a Master of Calligraphy and a teacher of his art both privately and at boys' and girls' schools, would often instruct the introductory classes. Master Uemura, from all reports, seems to have been in great favour with the ladies, having a refined and kindly manner. Both these instructors at the time held the then highest rank of 4th Dan. Master Uemura had not attended university, but had been a private student of Funakoshi for many years. Master Hironishi had graduated from Waseda University with a bachelor's degree in Russian language and literature.

Harada said that at that first lesson he remembers finding the movements and techniques *"very, very difficult"*. Smiling, he also noted that he was the only male student in the beginners' group, for girls from a local Middle School were training there as part of their physical education, their school having been closed down as a result of the war. Most of these girls simply dressed in light, loose-fitting clothing to train, but some wore *hakama* (divided skirts). There were no changing facilities at the Shotokan as such, and the girls came already appropriately clothed. The boys and

Women's self-defence at the Shotokan dojo.

men changed in the dojo itself, hanging their clothing up on pegs as one entered the dojo, or if these were full, placing their belongings in neat piles upon the *tatami* (straw mats). The men changed in the dojo irrespective of whether the girls and women were present. Mitsusuke thoroughly enjoyed his first lesson and decided that Karate was for him. He had to pay an enrolment fee, and then on an advanced monthly basis for his training. Harada recalls that the costs were very reasonable.

He would catch the train from his home in the Shakugi district to his school, and after his studies catch another train to the Shotokan dojo, which was about forty minutes away from his home and ten minutes from school. The Shotokan, from which Funakoshi's style (almost certainly the most practised in the world today) was later to be named, was actually very small in size and rectangular in shape. Harada compared it to a badminton court. The dojo floor was of a very hard, dark wood, unpolished, yet showing a beautiful grain. Great care was taken with the floor, and after each lesson it would be swept, and students would wash it in water and then run up and down on all fours with rags to dry it. The evening class, with an average of about 20 students, lasted two hours, from seven to nine o'clock, and Harada remembers that training was not very demanding, not very taxing at all, and consisted of practice in *kata* (forms), *kihon* (basics) and *kumite* (sparring), especially s*anbon kumite* (three-step sparring).

The '*Ten no Kata*' (Kata of the Universe) was practised assiduously. Devised by Master Funakoshi, the '*Ten no Kata*', which is not practised as widely as it might be today, is a set of ten 'units' performed on both sides (making 20 in all). From the informal attention stance, the Karate-*ka* (student) moves forward four times and backward six times, always returning to the same mark. On the movements backward, a partner may be used. Only a very small area is required in order to practice, and this type of training is especially appropriate for group practice in a small dojo similar to the confined space of the Shotokan. Designed for beginners, Master Funakoshi recommended that the '*Ten no Kata*' be practised seriously and diligently until it became part of one. The techniques covered are two types of punch, six types of block, and one type of strike. Techniques are spread over the three levels: *jodan* (upper level), *chudan* (middle level) and *gedan* (lower level). Four stances are practised in all.

Each punch or strike is accompanied by an intense *kiai* (expression of vital spirit — much more than just a yell) and blocks followed by counters are eventually performed as one continuous action, allowing the opponent no time for escape. The 20 'units' of the '*Ten no Kata*' should, by Master Funakoshi's reckoning, take about two minutes to perform (presumably when you engage with a partner for the *ura* {reverse} section of the kata, otherwise the time suggested seems overly long).

Because Japan was at war and there was a constant fear of air raids, a black-out had to be observed. The black curtains in the dojo were always pulled in the evening, and the electric lights inside were often minimal, sometimes to the extent that Harada couldn't see what the student next to him was doing. The atmosphere in the dojo, as a result of the pulled curtains, which restricted air flow, and the humidity, was often so stifling that one could hardly breathe. If the siren went, practice would stop immediately, and everyone would get changed as quickly as they could. The lights would be turned off completely, and they would turn on the radio in the pitch-dark dojo and listen to reports of the incoming aircraft. Harada can also remember the first time he saw black-belts train at the dojo. They performed the kata '*Kanku Sho*' as part of their practice, and Harada was greatly impressed.

Master Harada recalled that the ease of training in late 1943 did not change significantly in 1944 and 1945 during the evening sessions, despite liberal journalism to the effect that, due to the possible threat of invasion, training became very severe at the Shotokan at that time. Based almost exclusively on an interview with a particular senior Karate-ka, the training he supposedly underwent was conducted during the daytime, so there is room for doubt, and the point needs further research. However, Master Harada said that he heard no rumours at all about any intensive training where, so it is reported, individuals died and suffered terrible injuries, such as the loss of an eye. "*What? At the Shotokan… No!*" was Harada's reply. It seems likely that the truth is a lot less sensational than some would have us believe. Training during the war years at the Shotokan was probably as focused as one would expect today, especially when the black-belts practised. It is said that this group concentrated mainly on basics, one-step sparring and semi-free sparring.

It is, however, quite true that with the threat of invasion,

'Waka Sensei' and 'Ro Sensei' (young teacher and old teacher)...as Yoshitaka Funakoshi (left) and his father, Gichin, were affectionately known at the Shotokan.

numbers in the Shotokan swelled so that students were practising in the street outside. The dojo, Harada recalls, could hold about 40 students, but things were very cramped. Certainly Harada remembers that training did hot-up considerably on the occasions when university students visited the Shotokan. Training and gradings were very hard, and sometimes the white-belt university students would thrash the Shotokan black-belts in kumite. It must be remembered, however, that there were only two belts operating at this time, white and black, and it is most likely that these 'white-belts' were probably of 1st *Kyu* (grade below *Dan* [black-belt] level) standard and shortly would take their *Shodan* (1st level of black-belt rank) examination. Master Funakoshi would apparently get very upset at the news because the type and ferocity of training was viewed as an aberration of true practice. It is strange, therefore, when one reads that Funakoshi, along with his son, Yoshitaka and Shigeru Egami, were supposedly responsible for the intensive training mentioned above, and questioned by Harada.

Harada also remembers well the first time the legendary Yoshitaka Funakoshi came to the Shotokan dojo when he was training. One of the black-belts had informed the class that 'Waka Sensei' was coming, and everyone eagerly awaited his arrival. Yoshitaka, sometimes referred to as Gigo (from the Chinese), Gichin's third and youngest son, was often affectionately called 'Waka Sensei' (young teacher) to differentiate him from his father, who used to be referred to as 'Ro Sensei' (old teacher). Yoshitaka was Chief Instructor to the Shotokan and first assistant to his father after the sudden death of Master Takeshi Shimoda. Due to lack of medicine, Shimoda died in a few short days of pneumonia, in 1934. Yoshitaka, too, had been awarded the title of *Renshi* from the Butokukai, and held the rank of 4th Dan. Of all the Shotokan Karate-ka of that period, only Yoshitaka, for certain, held *Renshi*. He lived with his wife and family next door with his father (and later, toward the end of the war, Harada believes, his mother joined them from Okinawa). Harada remembers that Gichin and Yoshitaka's names were on their gate, so that the postman would know where they lived. Yoshitaka adored his father and the old master had complete faith in his son. They would often joke with one another about the correct method of practice, and Harada remembers his seniors saying that Yoshitaka once said, laughingly, "*You do not want to train with my father — he is too old,*" but everyone knew that it was tongue-in-cheek.

The important initial impressions that Harada had of Yoshitaka were both psychological and physical. As he bowed and entered the dojo the atmosphere changed, becoming charged with energy — he projected an air of self-confidence and authority. "*It was because of his personality,*" Harada said. "*He had a crew-cut, large eyes and a prominent hara*" (abdomen: more specifically the region about two inches below the navel that, according to traditional Japanese thought, is a person's spiritual centre). What was particularly strange at the time was his noticeably soft body, which seemed a complete paradox given his awesome ability and reputation. He was 36 years old. Certainly, Yoshitaka was more stocky and taller than his father at about 5ft. 4ins. Master Harada has discerned three types of Karate-ka, based upon their personality. Yoshitaka is classed as Type 1 — a member of a small and selective group who were both

"When Master Yoshitaka Funakoshi entered the dojo, the atmosphere changed, becoming charged with energy"...

physically and psychologically strong, technically excellent and spiritually advanced. Harada believes that such individuals are born with such a predisposition which evolves and shines through the practice of Karate-Do. Examples of Types 2 and 3 are referred to later.

During the day Yoshitaka worked as an X-ray technician for the Ministry of Health at Tokyo's Imperial University and the Ministry of Education, a position he was able to take up as he had studied photography at technical college. He never interfered with the practice going on in the dojo, but would quietly train on his own in a corner. To the left, as one entered the Shotokan, was positioned a large, full-length portable mirror. Yoshitaka would examine his form in great detail in this mirror. Harada, and other students, would do likewise prior to the commencement of their class. At the end of the lesson, Yoshitaka would call over selected black-belts and practice pre-arranged sparring with them. Yoshitaka was very much concerned with

Master Yoshitaka Funakoshi (left) and Master Shigeru Egami [who features prominently later in this book] engage in one-step sparring in a series of photos taken at the Shotokan (circa 1940).

reality and sometimes would instruct his black-belt juniors to strike him in unrehearsed and non-specified attacks with punches and kicks. He would stand in a deep and dynamic *fudo-dachi* (rooted stance), his favourite stance which Harada believes he devised from a *kiba-dachi* (straddle-legged stance) from the *'Tekki'* kata, with an open-handed *kamae* (posture) guard. The black-belts would be palmed away by Yoshitaka with such (controlled) force that few chose to partner him willingly. He would also welcome free and forceful attacks with the *bokken* (wooden sword) and *bo* (staff), and whilst his *tai sabaki* (body evasion) was of the first order, he did not always escape injury, indeed Harada remembers Master Egami telling him of the bruises that Yoshitaka suffered and of the scars he bore from this practice.

Yoshitaka only ever practised with black-belt students that he liked and who showed effort. As an example of this, Harada

Master Yoshitaka Funakoshi (left) and Master Egami demonstrate applications from the 'Heian' and 'Tekki' kata (above and on the next facing page).

remembers a High School pupil who went to Yoshitaka at the end of the lesson and asked if he could practice with him. Yoshitaka, who never lost his temper (unlike his father, who sometimes did), and who was always most courteous, replied: "*Perhaps another day*". On one occasion, when there were atypically two lines of students rather than the usual one (the difference was as a result of another group of young women who trained that day), Harada was kicking at head-height with all the determination and power he could muster. Unfortunately, the kick was too high and its momentum took his supporting leg away, with the embarrassing consequence that he landed rather indelicately on the wooden floor in the middle of the dojo opposite the shrine. Yoshitaka, smiling from ear to ear, came over to him, clapped and said: "*Good effort. Yes, well done*". Yoshitaka understood. One can feel fairly certain that if Harada had been a black-belt at the time, he would have had the honour of practising with Yoshitaka. Harada recalled that a friend and classmate's father (the boy did not train), whose surname was Ushiama, was a close friend of Yoshitaka.

Sometimes, even though expected, Yoshitaka did not come to the dojo. It was only later that Master Harada found out that Yoshitaka was so very ill. Harada explained that when Master Hironishi told him of 'Waka Sensei's' condition, he was really shocked, because he looked so fit and strong. Yoshitaka died in November 1945, leaving a wife and family. Harada said that he died not, as is commonly believed, of tuberculosis (which had been diagnosed at the age of seven, when doctors said that he would be unlikely to live beyond 20), nor leukaemia (as has been reported elsewhere), but of gangrene of the lungs. This was, and still is, a particularly unpleasant way to die, and no doubt brought about as a function of Yoshitaka's tuberculosis and the terrible conditions after the war (though the condition invariably follows pneumonia when the individual is in a serious debilitated state). A portion of the lung dies and putrefies, and when spat up there is a most appalling smell.

Master Harada could only describe Yoshitaka's untimely death as a disaster of the first order for Shotokan practice, and one poorly understood by the Shotokan community throughout the world. The author asked Harada what he thought would have happened if he had not died. He replied that many of the Japan Karate Association (JKA) seniors would not have occupied places of such prominence. Yoshitaka would have been their senior, knew who was who, and would ask: *"What are you claiming?"* One world-famous master, now dead, did not actually practice that hard in his younger days, and acted as the cheerleader for his university in Sumo matches and so on. He apparently only learned Karate to build up an image so that the individuals under him, in his capacity as cheerleader, would do as he asked. Harada said that Yoshitaka would also not have permitted freestyle competition. He last saw Yoshitaka in February 1945, and learned of his death, at the age of 39, from a small obituary that appeared in a number of newspapers. Yoshitaka's funeral was held on the 24th November 1945, less than three months after the Japanese surrender.

Today, Yoshitaka is remembered as a shadowy figure, made

Master Egami (on the left of each photo) attacks
whilst Master Yoshitaka Funakoshi defends.

more remote by the passing of time. Master Harada is one of the few people alive today who actually knew him. Yoshitaka was a towering, dynamic, creative and innovative Karate-ka, under whom much progress was made. Indeed, one might go as far as to say that he was largely responsible for developing the style Shotokan Karate-ka practise today. The knowledge that he had been given only a short time to live when young, motivated him to excel, and both technically and spiritually he had gone beyond others. As a result of hard training, he had outlived the doctor's diagnosis by 20 years. He was not liked by everyone, however, and Harada recalled one very senior grade, now in his eighties, calling him "*Yoshitaka San*" (Mr.) instead of the customary "*Yoshitaka Sensei*" (teacher —though literally 'one who has gone before').

Yoshitaka Funakoshi's major legacy was the stressing of the importance of using the whole body in a co-ordinated manner, exploring the tremendous value of relaxation, and the value that could be gained from strong, supple hip flexors and deeper, longer and more grounded stances (as Shimoda had done). He moved like a tiger, with grace yet having great power in reserve. He was instrumental in developing, amongst other techniques, *mawashi-geri* (roundhouse kick), which he practised with *tsumasaki* (the tips of the toes), *ushiro-geri* (back kick), *yoko-geri* (side-kick) and *fudo-dachi* (rooted stance), which, as I have noted before, is believed to be an adaptation of *kiba-dachi* (straddle-legged stance) rather than *zenkutsu-dachi* (front-stance). The development of a new stance required great courage as it was a break with tradition. It is commonly reported that Yoshitaka occasionally broke the *makiwara* (striking post) which he achieved with *gyaku-zuki* (reverse punch), from a completely relaxed base. He would take up *kiba-dachi* and swiftly shift into *fudo-dachi*, using the weight change and power of the fast hip movement to perform this impressive feat. However, what is not so well known is that quite a few other Karate-ka also broke the *makiwara* at that time.

As one entered the gate leading to the Shotokan building, there was the option of turning either left or right. Left, as already mentioned, led to the Funakoshi residence, and right would take one to the dojo. Facing the dojo entrance from out-side, on the right of the path were two or three makiwara, the posts of which were set in the ground. Makiwara in those days

Master Yoshitaka Funakoshi training on the makiwara (striking post).

were of the correct type — not too thick (about half a centimetre) at the top, tapered to a square base of some 12 centimetres in width and 12 centimetres in depth. Harada saw Yoshitaka strike the makiwara, and tried to imitate what he had seen. He would remove the upside-down bucket that protected the striking area from the elements and place it on the ground, practice hard, and then replace the cover. Gichin Funakoshi would also hit the makiwara at the Shotokan dojo, though Harada never saw him. It is said that the old master would strike the post one thousand times a day, left and right lightly, uttering a soft *"Hoi"* sound. Harada said that later, when he knew

*Masters Wado Uemura (left), Yoshiaki Hayashi (centre) and Yoshitaka
Funakoshi outside the entrance to the Shotokan.*

the master, Funakoshi's punches did not seem strong to an
observer, but were, in fact, very powerful.

Harada recalled that Masters Hironishi, Uemura and
Yoshitaka were good teachers and encouraged their students, but
he found Master Yoshiaki Hayashi, who also held the rank of 4th
Dan, not to be in the same mould. Tall, slim and technically very
good, Hayashi, who worked as a clerk in a chemical company
(after the war he became a director of the firm), was less than
encouraging. Harada performed the kata *'Taikyoku'*, but not to
Hayashi's liking, and the teacher told his student that he had
demonstrated the kata like a girl, so he had better go and train
with them. This Harada did for the rest of the lesson, but he
disliked Hayashi after that, for he considered the reaction
uncalled-for and lacking respect for a student who was trying his
best. Master Harada later classified Master Hayashi as a Type 2
personality — characterised by the ability to lead and technically superior, but not spiritually strong, *"not like a Buddhist
priest"*. In fact, Hayashi's direction was technically rather point-
less, as the training for the women was the same as for the men

and they paired-up together. Harada remembers two or three female black-belts, especially Akiko Heibino. She used to wear a *gi* (uniform) and changed in Funakoshi's house prior to the lesson. Harada recalled her performing kata in particular, but also basic self-defence techniques.

Harada remembers that Master Hironishi used to train at the Shotokan dojo virtually every evening, but Uemura, Hayashi and Yoshitaka sometimes would all be there at the same time. This was always a cue for a good evening's training, as the class would be split up, though, as previously mentioned, Yoshitaka only ever taught black-belts, and the instructors would explain technique and theory in great detail. During the war, Harada would train at the Shotokan three or four times a week, though he never actually saw Gichin Funakoshi at this time. Masters Hayashi, Uemura and Yoshitaka all helped Master Funakoshi to compile and edit '*Karate-Do Nyumon*'.

In the early morning, between 2.00 and 3.00 a.m., on the 10th March 1945 (and not the 29th of April as has previously been recorded), the Shotokan dojo and the adjoining Funakoshi residence were completely destroyed by fire in a truly horrendous air raid which began about midnight, involving some 280 B29 bombers. The entire centre of Tokyo, an area of 40 square kilometres, was devastated. The American planes flew in from Guam, attacked in waves, and suffered very minor losses. The wooden Shotokan simply burned away, leaving nothing but ashes, broken and distorted glass, shattered and discoloured roof tiles. It had been an extremely windy night, and the gusts had fuelled what was the worst conventional air-raid in the world's history. Master Funakoshi later wrote that he considered the establishment of the Shotokan to have been the most wonderful achievement that he had accomplished in his life, and Egami wrote that its destruction must have been a terrible blow to Yoshitaka.

One thousand, six hundred and sixty-five tons of bombs and incendiaries fell that fateful night. The bombing arrangement was such that an incendiary was delivered approximately every 100 feet, and these were interspersed with high-explosive bombs that charged the flames. This one raid alone killed some 100,000 people (figures vary), and for the next three days, from eight in the morning until five in the evening, Harada helped to collect and load the badly-charred bodies of men, women and children on to lorries. The smell of burned flesh and the unrecognisable remains of his fellow-human beings is still with him, though as a 16-year-old he coped exceptionally well. Shrugging his shoulders and tilting his head to one side whilst gazing down, as though in full acceptance of the inevitability of it all, Master Harada said that he took the gruesome task of clearing the bodies in his stride. It was war, he was young, and you lived for the day. The bodies were taken to a central location and disposed of in a communal funeral pyre. But on to happier memories!

Harada said that he had thoroughly enjoyed his training at the Shotokan. After its destruction, students from the dojo trained in the gym of the Takada Dai Hachi Primary School. This school had closed down and the children had been evacuated to the country. Master Hironishi taught in the evenings at this dojo, but attendance was poor, only three, four or five students, and practice was exactly the same as at the Shotokan: kihon, kumite and kata ('*Taikyoku Shodan*'). Sometimes, Harada recalled, they did very little practice and Master Hironishi would tell them stories of his military exploits in China. In April 1945, a bomb exploded, narrowly avoiding the Harada family home. "*We were very lucky,*" he said.

After the Shotokan was destroyed, Harada wrote to Master Funakoshi asking whether it would be possible to continue training. Master Hironishi also wrote a letter of introduction to Funakoshi on Harada's behalf. Master Funakoshi, who was then living with his eldest son, Yoshihide, in Koishikawa, Tokyo, replied that Harada was welcome to train with him at his son's house on a private basis. Yoshihide had come to Japan prior to his father. Master Funakoshi, who had been training in Karate for some 67 years by this time, would accept no money for his tuition. The year was 1946. Harada would train for one hour, three or four times a week, though the old master wanted him to train every day. The lesson was normally held in the afternoon, at two or three o'clock, but sometimes at five or six. Master Funakoshi would mostly sit in *seiza* (formal kneeling position) with his back very straight, very correct, as was the custom. His teachers, Masters Azato and Itosu, had done the same before him. His hands would be open, palms down, and placed above his knees, which would be apart. He wore a light *kimono* called a *yukata*. Sometimes the old master would stand watching. He would not have a particular location in the dojo where he would

Master Gichin Funakoshi carefully observes a student's technique as he performs tameshiwari ('trial by wood').

be situated, but moved about observing from different angles.

The young Harada, who was attempting to enter university, practiced the kata 'Taikyoku Shodan' slowly, with no power, continuously. The lounge, which acted as a dojo, was very small, and the frail old wooden house would vibrate if a technique was done too powerfully. There was no furniture as such in the room. Conversation and encouragement were minimal, but Harada does remember that Funakoshi insisted on the *kiai* points being correctly observed. Once, Harada did not make the requested *"A"* (not *"Ah"*) sound on one of the two *kiai* points in the kata (this sound focuses the lower abdomen and is important), and produced a more shallow throat-orientated sound like a shout. Master Funakoshi, who always demanded a vigorous *kiai*, reprimanded him severely for this and was really rather angry. As the master wrote, *"Martial arts without kiai are like a person devoid of a soul"* ('Karate-Do Nyumon', Kodansha: 1988). Yet the atmosphere of that dojo was more friendly and informal with the old master looking on, when compared to the impersonal, militaristic teaching of the large classes that Harada was later to encounter. However, after three months of 'Taikyoku Shodan' and nothing else, of Master Funakoshi endlessly repeating: *"Mo ichi do...Hai!"* ("One more time...Yes!"), Harada ceased going to the lessons, explaining that it was unbelievably boring. The young 16/17-year-old did not speak or write to Funakoshi explaining that he would no longer be coming, something that Harada now feels embarrassed about. The unforgiving and repetitious nature of kata training that Master Funakoshi had been brought-up with under his own instructors more than 60 years before, and that he continued to teach, was simply no longer acceptable to the post-war Japanese, as he was later to discover.

"What did he expect from the old master?" the author asked. Harada, laughing as he replied to my question (he has a marvellous sense of humour), and the author must confess to laughing openly too, every time he thinks on Master Harada's manner of saying: *"I was expecting kumite or some special super power, but he didn't teach anything at all, not a stance, not a punch, not a kick, not a block"*. Occasionally, however, after practice, the old master, whose mind was then still very alert and his thinking clear, would sit down and give Harada some basic advice on self-defence. In his quiet and well-educated manner, Funakoshi would give his views on how to walk around a corner in case someone was waiting for you out of sight and ready to pounce, and so on. One piece of advice that particularly stands out in Harada's mind, was that if you think you are being followed, especially at night, walk at a regular pace and listen to the footsteps of the 'pursuer' behind you. Speed up, and see if his footsteps keep pace with yours. If they do, then you have been forewarned. *"Stories like this, O'Sensei used to tell,"* Harada said. Master Funakoshi would also talk about his youth on Okinawa and days of past national glories, such as when he saw the Baltic Fleet. This did not go down too well with the young Harada, however — after all Japan had just lost the war! Harada recalls that at this time Master Funakoshi did have another private student, for Harada saw him twice, but he never knew his name or what became of him. As fate would have it, Master Funakoshi and Harada were to renew their acquaintance a few years later, and their association was to last until the old master died.

The fact that Harada practised *'Taikyoku'* under Gichin Funakoshi is a particularly interesting, if esoteric point, for much debate has raged on the subject. Indeed, some noted authorities, including senior Japanese, most notably Masatoshi Nakayama, late Chief Instructor of the JKA, have questioned whether Master Funakoshi taught *'Taikyoku'* at all. The author has

Master Gichin Funakoshi demonstrates his proficiency with the bo (staff). Note the style of uniform and sash, tied at the side.

written quite a lot on this subject before and does not wish to repeat himself here, however, the new information that has come to light must be mentioned. Master Harada learned 'Taikyoku' at the Shotokan dojo under Master Hironishi. It is generally believed that Yoshitaka devised the kata (possibly with

Hironishi) under his father's watchful eye. Harada never actually saw Master Yoshitaka practice any kata at all. Master Gichin Funakoshi certainly claimed, in writing, to have devised the kata which were an outcome of his many years of study into Karate-Do at much the same time as he devised the *'Ten no Kata'*.

For readers who are not familiar with *'Taikyoku'*, sometimes referred to as *'Kihon Kata'* (Basic Kata), let me just say that it is composed of only twenty movements, and is the first form to be taught in a number of styles. There are eight *gedan-barai* (often translated as 'downward block', though actually, 'lower-level sweep') and twelve *oi-zuki* (lunge punches), all performed in *zenkutsu-dachi*. Translated as 'First Cause', *'Taikyoku'* has its philosophical and spiritual underpinning deeply rooted in Buddhism. Once the practised Karate-ka is fully aware of its theoretical relevance, the kata's basic and seemingly simple movements take on an advanced, not to say profound meaning. Hence Master Funakoshi's famous quote that: "*Upon the mastery of the art of Karate, an expert will return to select it as the ultimate training kata*" (*'Karate-Do Kyohan'*, Kodansha: 1973).

The author has written before that, as the high grade's black-belt, fraying by constant use, begins to return to whiteness, and thus toward the completion of the circle, so *'Taikyoku'* is the alpha-omega of forms.

For the first time in the West, at least as far as the author is aware, there is proof that Master Funakoshi taught *'Taikyoku Shodan'*. Not only did he teach the kata, however, he trained enthusiastically in it also (see next chapter). Harada noted that the kata was also definitely taught at the universities of Chuo (where Hironishi taught Karate), Toho and Gakushuin. After the Shotokan was destroyed, the kata was taught at Waseda University, but not at Takushoku (the university that was chiefly responsible for JKA instructors and the exporting of the Shotokan style).

It is worthy of note that Harada remembers quite clearly Master Funakoshi asking him, before the commencement of his first lesson, whether he knew *'Taikyoku'*. Once Harada indicated that he did, it seems evident that Funakoshi placed considerable value on the kata, for with the repetitive nature of his training he would presumably have wished to instil only that which he regarded as important in his young private student.

2

University
Days

The earliest photograph of Mitsusuke Harada in a Karate gi (uniform), aged 19. He is standing, far right, demonstrating a gedan-barai (lower-level sweep). Waseda University Summer Gasshuku (Training 'camp'), Sado Island, 1948.

After ceasing training under Master Funakoshi, Harada did not practise Karate for a short period. He was still interested in the art, but did not wish to restrict his training solely to kata. He wrote to Master Hironishi enquiring whether he could be taken on as a private student, but Hironishi replied that it was not possible as he did not have a dojo. Hironishi was at the time teaching at Chuo University, which had decided to change from Wado-Ryu to Shotokan in 1940. Originally the university had wanted Yoshitaka to teach, but he was unable to, so Master Toshio Kamata taught instead. Master Hironishi still teaches Karate at Chuo despite being in his eighties. If Harada was genuinely interested in pursuing Karate, Hironishi suggested that he should view the training at his intended university — Waseda. In June 1947, at the end of the first semester, Harada sat and watched a class at the university dojo. *"It was completely different, gohon kumite* (five-step sparring) — *bang. All the beginners were being hit by the black-belts, I was really scared. Oh! That's enough — so I didn't go again."*

In April 1948, Harada entered Waseda, following his father before him, to embark initially upon a three-year bachelor's degree in commerce. After one year on the course, however, the degree programme was changed to the American system. This meant that he had to start afresh on a new four-year degree. Thus Harada's first degree took five years. This unforeseen change put a considerable and understandable strain upon the family's resources. Yutaka had sold family property to pay for his son's education (Waseda, like other Japanese universities, was a private institution), but Harada had to work in the holidays and his spare time. Temporary jobs ranged from acting as barman and glass washer to a caretaker for the American Navy and Airforce. Commerce was not, however, Harada's first-choice subject. He was particularly interested in history and literature, but had not achieved sufficient grades to read for a degree in either of these fields. Harada commuted from his home daily to attend lectures.

When his father had returned to Waseda, he was very disappointed that nobody had remembered him, so he suggested to his son that he become actively involved in some physical activity and to try to excel so that his name would be remembered. Yutaka encouraged his son as much as possible for the thought of his own father's initial lack of encouragement was still with him. Perhaps, not that surprisingly, after what he had witnessed the year before, the study of Karate was not an imme-diate choice. Rather, Harada tried to join the basketball course, but was deemed too short. It was only then, with some consider-able hesitation, that he signed up for the Karate club, which was much respected among the Tokyo universities. He had not trained for over a year and now, nine months after being terrified by the aggressiveness and overwhelming intensity of training he had witnessed as a spectator, he was there amongst them.

Some of the more senior grades had been *kamikaze* ('divine wind') suicide pilots, spared their death by Japan's surrender on the 2nd September 1945. Only a few months before the end of the war, 3,000 of their comrades had died in suicide attacks during the Battle of Okinawa, sinking 21 ships and damaging a further 66. These individuals had now come back to Waseda to conclude their studies, and sometimes they took the lessons, for some were black-belts, in a very militaristic fashion. Harada remembers that at the beginning of the very first lesson he had, all the new boys (no women) were lined up and asked their name and their motive for training. Many said that they wanted to 'smash' (Harada's word) the opposition, and he wondered if he had done the right thing by opting for Karate! Unfortunately, he let slip that he had trained at the Shotokan, and thereafter became a 'marked man', because all the students, black-belts included, wanted to test him. Amongst his numerous injuries was a broken nose — "*Everyone had their nose broken, even Ohshima,*" Harada recalled. But injuries were not desperate, because he offered no confrontation with these black-belts — in other words he managed to escape their attacks, but he never shirked from partnering them. Harada remembers that the training camps and week courses were very demanding, and he did not enjoy them at all. At the end of the first week's (beginners) course that he attended, held in January 1949, he was graded to 5th Kyu by Master Hiroshi Noguchi and Master Toshio Kamata (Watanabe), under the watchful eye of Master Funakoshi.

Master Kamata had had a dangerous yet most interesting war. Graduating from the famous Nakano School, he became a Major, spying in Burma, helping the Burmese fight for independence. He married a General's daughter, and was later rewarded by the Burmese Government. At Waseda, he had been captain of the Karate club for two years, a rare achievement, and the team had gained a great reputation under his leadership. Master Kamata

Hiroshi Kamata (Captain of Waseda University Karate Club) and
Matsuo Shibuya (Vice-Captain). Sado Island, 1948.

later changed his surname to his wife's family name, Watanabe.

Whilst at university, students would rise early to be ready for training at six in the morning for three hours before university lectures started on these one-week courses. *"No-one would fail the grading. All the beginners would be given a special diploma,"* Harada recalled. At Waseda, the grading ladder started at 7th Kyu, but different universities operated different systems and there was no common policy.

Harada would frequently collect Master Funakoshi by taxi and escort him to the Waseda dojo. On the 1st May 1949, the day the *Nippon Karate Kyokai* (Japan Karate Association) was formed, Harada was asked by the dojo Captain, Joji Takada, to collect Funakoshi from his son's house and bring him to the meeting. Harada duly obeyed, but had not enough money for a taxi, so went by tram. They were already late, but on the journey back to the university Funakoshi suddenly grabbed his young minder by the arm (Harada said, interestingly, that he could still feel Funakoshi's impressively strong grip, for which the old master was noted) and rushed off the tram, with Harada protesting, being reluctantly dragged behind him. There in front of them was a cake shop! Funakoshi loved cakes, but apparently was rationed at his son's home, so he took advantage of the opportunity. Laughing, Harada recalled how the old master untied his *furoshiki* (a piece of cloth resembling a large handkerchief)

Group photo following the last practice at the Waseda Summer Gasshuku, Sado Island, 1948. Harada is seated third from the right, front row.

where he kept some personal possessions (Funakoshi disliked banks and apparently never used them, preferring to keep his worldly wealth, which was minimal, with him), saying: "*I have money, I have money*", found his purse and paid for the cakes, and promptly sat down to eat them. These were *manju* cakes, which are steamed, and are rather chewy, with a sweet, date-like taste, having the consistency of a dumpling. Funakoshi had ordered enough cakes for two people, but Harada could not eat his share because he was so worried about being late. Harada's plea that they should not waste a minute longer went largely unheeded, but eventually the master folded the remaining cakes, those that Harada had been unable to eat, up in his cloth, knotted it, and they were on their way again. Harada explained that the founding of the Japan Karate Association was about to commence, there was to be a uniting of Karate-ka after the disruption of the Pacific War, and there, apparently oblivious to the importance of events, was Funakoshi gorging himself like a child!

They finally arrived at the Iomiuri Shibum Hall just in time, or at least Harada had thought so, but Master Hironishi, who was instrumental in bringing everyone together, was furious. Harada said that it had been a last request of Yoshitaka to Hironishi to try to keep the 'Way of Shoto' alive if it was at all possible.

Trial by wood — a student breaks 2 inches of wood with mae-geri (front kick). Just visible behind him is Harada.

Although the inaugural meeting for the formation of the new association was to commence at 6.00 p.m., there had been a meeting prior to that to dissolve the old groupings. In all the preparations, the Waseda dojo Captain had not been informed of the earlier meeting, and consequently had not told Harada. Master Funakoshi knew nothing about it either! But all went well at the six o'clock meeting (and for a short period thereafter!), and a Karate demonstration followed in the evening, with Kichinosuke Saigo (who had trained at Funakoshi's original Meisei Juku dojo) the new Chairman of the JKA, naturally attending. It was at this demonstration that Harada saw, for the first time, Master Funakoshi perform an individual kata — 'Kanku Dai'. Harada subsequently saw the master demonstrate this form on other occasions, and remembers one fine performance at the Japanese Budo Sai in particular.

Harada recalled that the trips in the taxis were usually very interesting, though he remembers feeling really disappointed that sometimes the old master could not even recall his student's name. When he did remember, he always said *"Harada San"* (Mr. Harada), as was his custom. Master Funakoshi was fully aware

A demonstration of Jiyu Kumite (free sparring) at Waseda Univ. in 1951.

that his memory was not what it had been, for he openly admitted this to readers in his autobiography, 'Karate-Do: My Way of Life'. In 1949, Funakoshi was a frail 81-year-old. His wife had died of asthma in the late autumn of 1947 at Oita, in north-east Kyushu, their union lasting almost 60 years. Yoshitaka, in so many ways his father's hope for the future, was, of course, dead, and Funakoshi was attempting to correct the decline in the level of technique and the spiritual void that became so dominant as a result of the war. Yes, he was getting forgetful, that is, after all, an old man's prerogative, but the master had much to think on.

Now that Harada was at university, Funakoshi was much more communicative and friendly, and would often joke, though he was very quiet by nature. (Master Shigeru Egami did, however, say that he had seen Funakoshi lose his temper more than once in the Thirties). But Harada said that the old master lived in the past, always reflecting back on Okinawa, his Karate teachers, and the days of his youth, long before the 20th century had dawned. With all that had happened over the previous four years, perhaps the past was the best place for the old master's mind to be. He would say to his young student: *"This is how Itosu/Azato* [Harada cannot remember which] *could stop a man,"*

Master Gichin Funakoshi outside Waseda University.

and Funakoshi would lightly touch Harada with an *ippon-ken* (one-knuckle fist) on the chest. At the time Harada could not believe it, "*But now I understand*". The technique was soft, relaxed and unfocussed. Another story he would repeat, and it is now well known for Funakoshi wrote of it, was that Master Azato had techniques that really were like a sword and that would actually cut the skin, whilst Master Itosu had trained his body so that all punches and strikes would simply bounce off. To Harada there seemed an important inconsistency in this story, after all, how can honed weapons simply bounce off human flesh? This contradiction sowed the seeds of a lifetime search for *kime* (focus), which was shortly to be given a tremendous boost, courtesy of Master Egami. However, of this sword and shield story too, Harada now says that he understands.

Harada trained with Master Funakoshi from 1949-1952. The lesson the master took at Waseda was on Saturdays, noon to 1.30 p.m. Harada recalled that the university dojo was above ground level and Funakoshi, although fiercely self-reliant, had great difficulty climbing the stairs and needed help. He always, in later years, was supported by a cane walking-stick which he carried in his right hand. In fact, Harada recalled that Funakoshi, who would invariably wear a black *kimono*, trilby hat, and tall, heavy iron *geta* (clogs), would walk so very, very slowly unaided, but because they were often late, he needed aid to get to the university dojo in time. He would wait for every car and bicycle to go by before walking across a road, for example, and this would often take ages.

Before every lesson, Master Funakoshi would tell the same short story to his students. The tale, which was based on historical fact, put briefly, went as follows: Some five hundred years ago the island of Okinawa was split into three kingdoms: Chuzan (Middle), Nanzan (South) and Hokuzan (North). They were continually at war with one another, but eventually the Middle Kingdom won and united the island. Master Funakoshi literally told the story so often, sometimes after training as well, that the students referred to Saturday training as "*Chuzan, Nanzan, Hokuzan day*". This was very strange at the time, Harada said, but as a Karate allegory it is very clever, Picture the beginner, for which this story was intended, arms and legs lacking unified co-ordination. It is only when one learns to move from the hips, with the focus on the abdomen, that power begins to come.

Sparring practice outside the Kyudo (archery) dojo at Waseda in 1948.
Harada (front left) is partnered by Shoji Komori.

As was his custom, Funakoshi would teach only kata. Funakoshi believed that the kata were the soul of Karate, and that kihon and kumite were an aid to kata and not, as is commonly the interpretation today, the other way around. The consequent effect of this was that only five or six students would attend his lessons. These were almost always white-belts, who were required to attend a certain number of lessons in order to attain their course credit. Harada said that he thought the old master was very disappointed by the poor turn-out, but the black-belts wanted more — they wanted kumite. *"We didn't realise the importance of kata then...and Funakoshi didn't explain, and that's where he made the mistake. We, as students, were concerned with the second dimension, he* (Funakoshi) *spoke in the third."* ('*Conversations With Karate Masters*', Ronin: 1988). The problem of low turn-outs occurred at the other universities that Funakoshi taught at as well, such as Keio, Hosei, Chuo, Hitotsubashi and Gakushuin, the Nippon Medical College, Nikaido College of Physical Education, and the military and naval academies, amongst others, by all accounts. Master Harada explained that these lessons could sometimes be quite embarrassing, for the old master would appear naive and child-like.

Harada said he actually learned very little technically from these sessions. Funakoshi would often just watch practice from

the side of the dojo, though sometimes he would join in. If a
senior grade was instructing in kumite and Funakoshi was watching, he would no longer take any interest in the class, but turn
and look out of the window. *"This is how we knew O'Sensei
disapproved,"* Harada said. When the instructor understood
Funakoshi's reaction, he would return to kata practice and
Funakoshi would renew his interest and watch again. Harada
recalled that Funakoshi would insist that the students perform
the kata *'Taikyoku Shodan'* every lesson, and the master would
also practice the kata slowly with the class. (Harada never saw
him teach or perform *'Taikyoku Nidan'* or *'Taikyoku Sandan'*.)
*"He would always ask us to make sure that we finished our kata at
the point where we had begun it,"* Harada recalled. This form of
practice went on for three years. Occasionally, they would also
practice a *'Heian'* kata. Often Funakoshi would stop the class
and quote a maxim. Harada remembers that, *"Don't make
unnecessary enemies"* was one of the old master's favourites.

Once Funakoshi told the story of how he was sitting on a train
with his trilby occupying the seat next to him. A young rough
came into the carriage and sat on the seat, completely squashing
Funakoshi's hat. Never angry in such situations, Funakoshi
calmly asked the youth if he could have his hat back, and
avoided a potentially unpleasant scene. *"Stories like this he would
tell,"* Harada said. How to eat safely with chopsticks (in case
someone tried to ram them into your mouth) was another, and
he also mentioned how girls, if out after dark, should seek an
escort if they had to negotiate a lonely part of town — simple,
practical, sound advice. Today, Master Harada offers similar
advice to his students. *"At a bar, don't talk about Karate,"* being a
sensible favourite.

However, one thing that Harada will never forget about
Funakoshi was the change in physical appearance that came over
the master when he had his *gi* on. Funakoshi would change with
the rest of the students in the filthy changing rooms. The state of
these rooms always came as a great surprise to Funakoshi, but
no-one ever attended to them. Often they were so crowded that,
after training, Harada would visit the public baths for a bit of
peace and cleanliness. Harada said that Master Funakoshi would
take ages, as much as half-an-hour, to change, and they would
have to hurry him along as the dojo time was limited. When
Funakoshi walked into the dojo. *"It was quite remarkable,"* Harada

Group photograph on the Waseda campus, taken on the last day of mid-winter training in 1949. Master Funakoshi is seated in the centre of the middle row. Harada is on the back row, sixth from the left.

noted, as have other masters who trained under him. The old master seemed to straighten up and a glint entered his eye. *"It was a question of ki (spirit),"* Harada explained, *"something psychological... even Ohshima was very surprised"*. He was very agile despite his age and had an indomitable spirit — he would not shirk from kumite. Harada recalled that the master's favourite technique was to block *gedan-barai* on the inside of an opponent, catch the arm and unbalance his foe, and then deliver a one-knuckle punch to the head. At the first winter's course that Harada attended at Waseda, Master Funakoshi, despite being advanced in years, performed the above technique on the formal Master Kamata with impressive results. Though not a member of Waseda, Kamata had studied political economy at the university and was a founder of their Karate club. Nicknamed 'Small Kamata', he was very strict with himself and others, practised extremely hard and generated great power. He attacked Funakoshi with an *oi-zuki* from *zenkutsu-dachi*. The fragile old master, assuming a natural stance, blocked, pulled and countered

Group photo on the Waseda campus, 1950. Harada is standing third from the right. On the extreme right is Tsutomu Ohshima.

simultaneously, and Kamata fell to the floor. This caused a great impression all round. Harada's faith had been restored — Master Funakoshi could do it, and do it well. (Harada also recalled that Funakoshi would normally choose Master Isao Obata to pair-up with when demonstrating kumite at exhibitions).

Master Harada made it quite clear that it was Funakoshi's daily practice of kata that allowed him to continue training. His muscles had become properly attuned and he honed them each day with practice. It was only the continued practice of kata that allowed a Karate-ka to continue to be seriously active in both kumite and kata. Master Harada said that Master Funakoshi was a shining example of this.

Harada noted that Master Funakoshi was not highly regarded as a Karate-ka on Okinawa in the technical sense, but few would have questioned his character and intention. Master Harada has researched this subject — one of his sources being a very senior Karate-ka who is a friend of Gichin Funakoshi's sister's great-grandson. (The number of sisters Gichin had is unknown, though he was the only son.) Whilst Master Funakoshi was very highly regarded as an educator on Okinawa, the technical level of his Karate was considered quite poor. In Japan no-one really knew this, except Yoshitaka, who made the 1,000-mile trip back to Okinawa quite frequently. Yoshitaka's Karate technique was highly respected, but his *bo* technique was even more highly regarded by the Okinawans. Harada said that *bo* training should be used as physical practice for Karate-ka, the heavy staff building muscles in the correct way, but allowing the joints to relax. Harada believes that this shortcoming in Funakoshi's technique was one reason Yoshitaka trained so very hard. Although Yoshitaka's technique was completely different from that of his father, he could still say that he was Shotokan (which his father was proud of, after all, it was his creation).

Gichin Funakoshi's Karate had always been, and still was, very short and stiff. Yoshitaka had transcended this to produce a more flowing style. The simple truth is that father and son had different strengths. Later, when Harada was working in Brazil, an employee of the same bank but at another branch, heard that Harada practised Karate, and asked his instructor's name. When Harada replied that it was Gichin Funakoshi, the Okinawan response was: "*Your Karate not so good*". Similarly, Harada said that Master Kanken Toyama, a top pupil of Itosu and a similar age to Funakoshi, remarked that Funakoshi's personal Karate was poor. Karate is different things to different people, of course. Certainly the general belief was that Funakoshi was not as technically competent as Goju-Ryu founder Chojun Miyagi, for example, but is that really important? Funakoshi spent his life trying to improve himself and sharing his knowledge with others — what more can one ask? It is interesting to note that whilst there may be truth in Master Toyama's assertion, his own Karate completely disappeared. Toyama became headmaster of an infant school.

Information that has only recently come to light strongly suggests that when Funakoshi came to Japan in 1917 — in charge of the first officially-recognised demonstration of Karate on the Japanese mainland, held at the Butokuden (Martial

Virtues Hall) in Kyoto — he may well have known only one kata — 'Kushanku' ('Kanku Dai'), which he had learned from Master Yasutsune Itosu. Throughout his life, this remained his favourite form. Master Harada, who has been researching this problem also, believes that after the initial interest shown at this demonstration, Funakoshi had every intention of introducing Karate to Japan, and needed to learn more kata. He set about training at other masters' dojo, and learned the movements of various kata. He was not, however, confident in these newly-learned forms at all, and at the famous demonstration at the Kodokan in June 1922, under the watchful eye of Dr. Jigoro Kano (the founder of Judo) and an audience of over 100, he asked Shinken Gima to perform 'Naihanchi' ('Tekki') for example. As Harada put it, "This is a criticism of Funakoshi Sensei. He just learned the moves and that's why no-one trusted him" (that is, his rendition of certain kata). Funakoshi learned the 'Pinan' ('Heian') kata from Master Kenwa Mabuni (the founder of Shito-Ryu), who, of course, had learned them from Master Itosu. Harada remembers later, when in Brazil, he demonstrated 'Wanshu' ('Enpi') to some Okinawans, whose only comment was: "That is not real Wanshu".

Funakoshi changed moves in kata — he quite openly admitted it. There was nothing wrong with that, in the sense that other masters at the time were doing exactly the same thing. The motive was one of refinement. The old kata of Shotokan did not have any yoko-geri in them for example. Yoshitaka was responsible for their inclusion at the expense of mae-geri.

Despite more than 40 years passing, Harada noted that many of the things that Funakoshi had done or said were coming back to him now as truths, and that he was very grateful to Sensei. He described him as a truly great Karate master whom everyone (well, almost) respected. He noted that "It was a great pity that he didn't ask Funakoshi all the questions that he wanted to, but was unable to do so directly because of the very bad Japanese seniority system" ('Conversations With Karate Masters', Ronin: 1988). Harada continued that he would ask his seniors, but he didn't know if they could be trusted, and so how many of Funakoshi's ideas were communicated to the students through this seniority system he didn't know.

When Tsutomu Ohshima (who had come as a student from the Naval Academy) became Captain of the university Karate club — a very important position — in 1952, he insisted that all

Surrounding Master Gichin Funakoshi in this 1951 photograph are many outstanding Karate-ka. Second row: (left to right) Toshio Kamata, unknown, Hiroshi Noguchi, unknown, Master Funakoshi, Isao Obata, unknown, Masatoshi Nakayama, Takahashi (one of the best students of the 'modern style', according to Master Kase), Hidetaka Nishiyama, Taiji Kase. Back row: third from right, Tsutomu Ohshima.

the white-belts and all black-belts attend Master Funakoshi's lessons. (Captains of the Waseda team were, during Harada's undergraduate five years: 1948—Hiroshi Kamata; 1949 and 1950—Joji Takada; 1951—Kiyoshi Yamamiya; 1952—Tsutomu Ohshima; 1953—Kenjiryo Kawanabe). This had the effect of swelling the ranks to some 30-40 students. Many students at the time thought that Harada might have been Captain due to his earlier training at the Shotokan. Although secretly hoping the seniors might vote in his favour, Harada felt he stood only a very small chance, and was not really disappointed when his friend received the accolade. Under Ohshima (who studied political economy), the university club was very strong indeed with, at one time, four 3rd Dans, three 2nd Dans and five 1st Dans (which included Harada). The four 3rd Dans were Ohshima, Shoji Komory, Shuhei Endo and Teruhiko Okazaki (the elder brother of the famed JKA instructor Teruyuki Okazaki, 8th Dan, a long-time resident sensei in the USA).

Ohshima would collect Master Funakoshi regularly, but Harada remembers one particular occasion when he had to go. There was an important baseball match between the universities of Waseda and Keio, and all the students went along to cheer, but Harada was obliged to collect the old master. Harada, laughing, said that *"Ohshima could be very cruel"*. But in retrospect, I am sure readers will agree, he did Harada a considerable favour.

After training, Master Funakoshi would talk to a small group of students, of which Harada was always one, and then they took their teacher out for a meal. The old master was very happy at these times and would joke and tease the young Karate-ka. On one occasion, red-faced with *sake* (rice wine), which, because he rarely drank alcohol, would go straight to his head, he asked them how many times a week they had sex. On hearing their below-expectation replies, he told them to listen carefully, and instructed them on how many times they should engage in it for their age and for subsequent ages with regard to maintaining good health. What was particularly amusing about this story was that the old master got the recommendations completely the wrong way around! He also suggested certain delicacies that would improve their sexual appetite and performance. Unfortunately Harada cannot remember the food that the master spoke of!

Another story Harada remembers concerned the Japanese gods, Hacheman (the god of war) and Izumo (the god of weddings and sex). The story was how many times a week Hacheman's war horses could engage in sex. Izumo recommended four times a week. Hacheman replied that his horses were too busy to allow for that. Smiling, Funakoshi reflected on the comparisons between what the gods allowed for horses and men, and he said that human beings were obviously very lucky not to be as restricted as horses! The master really enjoyed his food and would concentrate upon eating, whilst the others sat around the table and talked. Sometimes he would take two hours to finish, and the students ended up ordering noodles for him so that he didn't take so long. Students from Keio though, apparently bought him a particularly delicious meal of eel and rice. Despite writing that he never drank alcohol, sometimes, as has been mentioned, Funakoshi would accept a small amount of *sake* or a single beer either during or at the end of the meal. When it was time to depart, Harada would often accompany the old master in the taxi home.

Outside the university dojo stood some ten striking posts. Harada would collect the key from the adjoining office and bring

Group photo taken at Shobara, 1952, following the Summer Gasshuku. Harada is kneeling third from the left, next to Tsutomu Ohshima (second from the left).

out the rice straw makiwara. He would practice his punches and strikes on these every day, normally for about twenty minutes to half-an-hour, before dojo training began at four o'clock, and sometimes after training. The seniors would often instruct the lower grades and watch their progress. At the first Summer School that Harada attended, the students were shown how to make a makiwara, and Harada built one in his garden at home. He would practice on it two or three times a week to supplement his university makiwara training.

During 1949 and 1950, Harada took part in much *kokan geiko* (exchange training) with members of other universities. The Waseda club would visit other university dojos and they in turn would visit Waseda. These exchanges, which were intended to benefit everyone by a mutual sharing of ideas, the showing of kata and so on, were normally held in the spring and autumn. Although practice was encouraged with other Shotokan dojos such as those operating at Keio, Chuo, Senshu (Harada remembers being very impressed by Taiji Kase's throwing techniques) and Takushoku, other styles of Karate were not neglected. Training with Kenwa Mabuni's Shito-Ryu from Kansai University (Harada also visited the Toho University dojo), and the Goju-

A farewell party in 1953 at a Japanese restaurant. Master Funakoshi is in the centre of the front row. Next to him (on the left) is Tsutomu Ohshima and Harada is on the far right of the second row.

Ryu dojos in the universities of Ritsumaiken and Doshisha in Kyoto, was actively encouraged.

These exchanges were sometimes rather brutal, as each member was determined to show off his university's strengths to maximum effect. As a consequence there were many injuries. What particularly impressed Harada was the technique of the Goju-Ryu practitioners, who would spar from *neko-ashi dachi* (cat-foot stance), from which they could kick easily. These Karate-ka would also invariably aim their strikes at the eyes, nose, and particularly vulnerable parts of the head, delivering *uraken* (back-fist) and *mawashi-zuki* (roundhouse punch) with great speed. Control was not always what it should have been and Harada once got caught with a strike on the temple, and, disorientated for a moment, collapsed. But he was all right — thankfully. Others from either side were not always so lucky, and Waseda certainly gave as good as they got.

At Keio, Harada watched Master Obata on one occasion perform the kata *'Kanku Dai'*, and Shuntaro Ito perform kumite. Of Ito, Harada recalled: *"He was very good, very strong"*. Both these men are now dead. Throughout his undergraduate days, the

A Meeting of Masters: this post-war period photo shows the Headmaster of Shito-Ryu, Kenwa Mabuni (centre left) and one of his senior students, Ryusho Sakagami (far left) greeting Gichin Funakoshi (centre right) at Osaka train station. Master Funakoshi had brought his students, Isao Obata (centre) and Masatoshi Nakayama (far right), to study the katas 'Gojushiho' and 'Nijushiho' under Master Mabuni.

Captains would urge the students to look at other styles. In 1948, for example, the entire Waseda University Karate club saw Hironori Ohtsuka, the founder of Wado-Ryu, at Nippon University. Master Ohtsuka was 55 at the time and had trained with Funakoshi for nine or ten years from 1923. Studying *Shindo Yoshin Ryu Jujutsu* from the age of five, he left Funakoshi and merged Karate with the more established art. Harada remembers the day as *"very interesting, and not so different"* (from what they were practising at Waseda at the time). Harada said that there was some small friction between Funakoshi and Ohtsuka. It was decided to ask Ohtsuka to leave, but Funakoshi was unwilling to really go through with it, as Ohtsuka was his student. Eventually, Yoshitaka had to ask him to leave. There was, however, nothing acrimonious about the parting. It was based purely on differences of opinion on technical matters in terms of what should be taught, and how. Master Ohtsuka, decorated for his services to the martial arts, died on the 29th January 1982, aged 89.

A personal friend and training companion of Ohshima was the famous JKA instructor Hidetaka Nishiyama, a previous Captain of Takushoku University. Master Nishiyama was invited to America by Ohshima in the late 1950s, which caused a few raised eyebrows, as it was thought that Ohshima would have chosen a graduate of Waseda. Nishiyama wrote, with co-author Richard C. Brown, 'Karate: The Art Of Empty-Hand Fighting'. Published in 1960, this book was in its 73rd printing ten years ago, and is still widely available. Anyway, Harada would pair up with Nishiyama, and many others of course, for kumite. Because the Waseda dojo was large, they could practice *gohon kumite* (five-step sparring), but the Takushoku University dojo was much smaller, and Harada recalls that they could practice only *sanbon kumite* (three-step sparring) there.

It was whilst a white-belt, though by today's grading a top brown-belt, that Harada achieved a feat that was to inspire great respect in all grades, including the senior black-belts. There was to be a Karate display by the universities and a demonstration of *tameshiwari* (literally, 'trial by wood'). (Harada first saw wood breaking at university, for none was done at the Shotokan dojo). Waseda agreed to break wood with *uraken*, known to be extremely difficult by the very nature of the technique, which relies on a snapping rather than thrusting motion. All the black-belts tried to break 2 one-inch (two-and-a-half centimetre) boards held together by colleagues, but none could succeed. Harada said that he would have a go. Two students held the two boards and both broke cleanly. Harada said that he had nothing to fear because the black-belts couldn't do it, so he wasn't expected to. He also noted that he felt nothing, no contact what-soever, when he broke the boards. Well, everyone was very surprised at Harada's accomplishment, and wanted to know how he had done it. He was then selected for the demonstration.

The display went on for some time before Harada had his moment. He and his two assistants took up their positions, and Harada struck the boards with his back-fist. The second board broke, but the first one remained intact (this is commonly the case, the reason for which is explained in the author's book 'Mysteries Of The Martial Arts'). Ohshima, who was one of two helpers, noticed that the first board had fractured, had a hairline crack through it, and quickly instructed Harada to strike the boards again. Thus the demonstration was a success, and Harada had proved that the first occasion he had broken the boards had not been a fluke. The author would strongly urge the reader not to try this type of break, for the only thing likely to be broken are

Personal practice: Harada tests his explosive power on a makiwara outside the Waseda University dojo. He would practice every day on the striking posts, normally for about 20 minutes to half-an-hour before dojo training began.

the knuckles! Harada said that this demonstration was his first and last, though later he did, in fact, break boards in Sao Paulo with *oi-zuki* and *mae-geri*.

In November 1951, Harada finally passed his 1st Dan, and wore the coveted black-belt. He had not really wanted to attempt this grading but Ohshima had encouraged him, for it was his last opportunity. It had been a tortuous experience, for he had failed his *Shodan* examination six (and not eight as previously recorded) times prior to succeeding. He said that he felt very ashamed at having failed so many times. Whilst readers will no doubt empathise with Harada's feelings, the author believes that the dedication he showed far outweighs any negative aspects that can be drawn from such failure. Indeed, the fact that Master Harada had so many attempts should be an inspiration to all those Karate-ka who fail a Dan grading a mere three or four times! After all, it doesn't really compare, does it? He had in the past presented 'Bassai Dai' kata for his grading (which was Master Noguchi's favourite form and the one he most frequently taught at the university). However, Ohshima said that he thought Harada was not really suited to that kata and so taught him 'Enpi' (a.k.a. 'Empi'), an ancient Shorin-Ryu form taught in the Tomari region of Okinawa and originally called 'Wanshu'. Harada passed with this kata, and 'The Flight of the Swallow', so-called because of its fast, sharp, light, 'high and low' techniques, became his favourite form.

Dan gradings were held twice a year by the JKA. Harada remembers that Masatoshi Nakayama (Takushoku University) and Kamata (Waseda University) had been in charge of kumite, and Masters Funakoshi, Hironishi (Chuo University), Hiroshi Noguchi (Waseda University) and Isao Obata (Keio University), the kata. All these senior instructors held the then highest rank of 5th Dan (JKA) at the time. Master Funakoshi was 'ungraded' as it were. Examiners in kihon were not regular, though Master Hironishi (who would often visit Waseda) often acted in this role, before he left the JKA. Harada's failing his Shodan six times was not completely his fault. As he said: "*I asked myself, 'What are they looking for? Which part is wrong?'*" The examiners, apparently, never gave him any indication. What compounded the problem was that different instructors from the different universities had diverse opinions as to what constituted correct form. Even at Waseda, different instructors were teaching

After 10 years of Karate, Mitsusuke Harada displays his muscular development at a friend's house in 1953.

different forms of the same style. Many of the most senior grades who attended the universities during the early Thirties had gone to the war or to China, and had stopped training. Their level of expertise had diminished, yet they kept their senior rank. This, Harada explained, was the Japanese hierarchical system at its weakest. The style they had left behind had undergone

considerable revision during the war, due mostly to much experimentation by Yoshitaka. Even a number of important new techniques had been interwoven into the art, such as *yoko-geri*
and *mawashi-geri*, of which they were ignorant. As Harada said,
this had the effect of retarding Karate's progress.

It was at Waseda that Harada came under the influence of two
additional and quite outstanding Karate masters, both of whom
deeply affected his life — Shigeru Egami and Tadao Okuyama.

Master Egami was born in 1912, in Fukuoka Prefecture, and
was a weak child. At Middle School he trained in Judo and
Kendo, which was customary. He attended Waseda University to
read for the bachelor's degree in commerce, studied some Aikido,
and helped to form the Karate club in 1931. His principal
teachers were Masters Gichin Funakoshi and Takeshi Shimoda.
Shimoda, a man of no great height, taught at the Waseda
University Karate club and was described by Egami as the most
talented of Funakoshi's students. He was an expert in the
Nen-Ryu school of Kendo and had studied *Ninjitsu* (the art of
invisibility). Egami could not block his teacher's 'light' punches
no matter how hard he tried. Egami also engaged a great deal in
'special practice' (as Harada put it) with Yoshitaka, his senior,
whom he described as being of excellent character and highly
skilled. Egami was an outstanding Karate-ka, generally regarded,
Harada said, as having the finest punch in the Shotokan style —
he was an *oi-zuki* specialist. Egami's enthusiasm for this technique and the manner in which he delivered it, so impressed
Harada that today the lunge punch is Harada's favourite
technique also. In contrast, the best kicker in the Shotokan style
was Master Morihana, a 4th Dan, who died in the war. *"Even
Noguchi very much respected Morihana,"* Harada recalled. Harada
believes he may well have seen this brilliant, yet forgotten,
Karate-ka during the war. Morihana attended Takushoku
University, which had student lodgings near where the Harada
family lived. Harada remembers seeing a tall man (Morihana
stood over six feet), very strong, practising side-kicks three or
four hundred times each side. *"I was very impressed,"* Harada said,
"I think this was Morihana".

A powerful, muscular, finely-attuned man after leaving
Waseda, Egami entered the Civil Service, but became dissatisfied
with this and subsequent positions. He saw National Service
before the war but contracted tuberculosis, and was excused

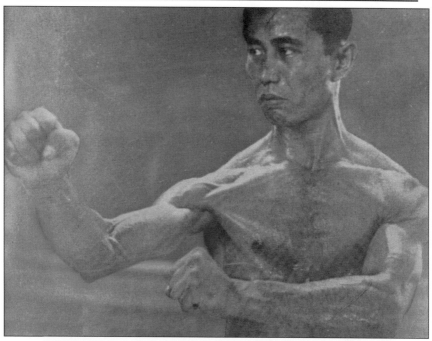

"Master Shigeru Egami was an outstanding Karate-ka, generally regarded as having the finest punch in the Shotokan style..."

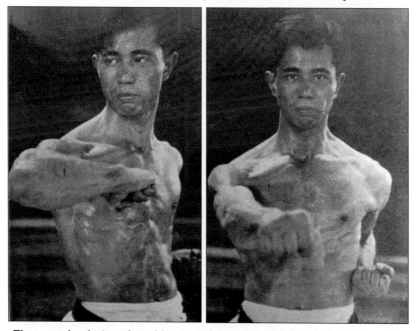

These early photos show his powerful and well-defined physique, prior to the onset of ill-health, from which he suffered for the rest of his life.

military service *per se* on health grounds, and was truly blighted by illness of various sorts for the rest of his life. Egami did, however, teach elements of Karate at the Nakano School. This school was for a unit of the special forces, a cross between Britain's MI5/MI6 and the SAS (Special Air Service). The eldest son in the Egami family had died, and Shigeru had been obliged to return to run a very large family construction company on Kyushu, building roads, embankments and so on, employing, Harada recalled, some two to three thousand men. The author understands that, how shall I put this, Egami was more honest and trusting than others, and the business encountered difficulties. He later lectured at Waseda in physical education and also taught Karate at the universities of Gakushuin, Toho and Chuo. He became President and Chief Instructor of the Shotokan of the Japan Karate-Do Shotokai.

Harada's first encounter with Master Egami, in 1954, was an unfortunate one. Harada had been asked to give moral support to his juniors by attending their Karate grading. The JKA grading was being conducted by Masters Funakoshi (who was in charge of the kata), Kamata and Nakayama (who were in charge of kihon), and Noguchi and Obata (who were in charge of kumite). However, due to torrential rain, Harada had unavoidably arrived a little late and the grading had begun. Master Egami, whom Harada, at that time, knew only by reputation, for his seniors were always talking about him, was sitting watching the grading (Egami was not JKA). When Harada arrived late, Egami, who had a very strong personality, reproached him severely (he appears to have been a fiery character who could lose his temper quite easily), so Harada retreated from a 'very bad atmosphere', with his 'tail between his legs'.

A few days later, Harada was practicing kata in the Waseda dojo alone, as he often did, and he felt a presence behind him. Master Egami (a 4th Dan) had entered and was standing there. Harada classes Egami as a Type 1 personality — the same as Yoshitaka. Egami asked him what he was doing. Harada was somewhat bemused, as it was fairly obvious that he was practising Karate, and did not answer. Master Egami touched Harada lightly on the shoulder and repeated his question: *"What are you doing?"* Harada replied that he was practising Karate. Egami said: *"Do you believe that this is Karate?"* to which Harada replied: *"Yes, I believe"*. Egami, shaking his head, said: *"That is not Karate"*. Now

Master Egami (left) and Master Hironishi sparring in 1936. These vintage photos were taken by Master Yoshitaka Funakoshi.

Harada was, to say the least, rather insulted, not to say annoyed, by this obvious slight upon his Karate practice. After all, he had not only trained at the Shotokan and been a private student of the founder of the style, but held black-belt grade as well! *"Let me feel your punch,"* Egami said, taking off his jacket (Egami had a reputation for such things). Harada assumed a *zenkutsu-dachi* and duly struck him in the abdomen with controlled force, using a reverse punch. The punch had no effect at all. *"I said let me feel your punch,"* Egami retorted. Harada, at this stage, decided to really punch, on the basis that, *'You asked for it'*. He took a step further back, deepened his stance and rushed in at Egami with a full-force *oi-zuki*. Just at the moment of impact, Egami thrust his body forward whilst tensing his considerable abdominal muscles. The force was such that Harada, instead of damaging Egami, flew backward, ending up spread-eagled on the wooden floor. Harada was most impressed by this demonstration, not only because he found himself on the floor, but that Egami was prepared to take the force of a black-belt's punch, something the other teachers (with the exception of Kamata) would apparently not do. *"What is your name?'* asked Egami. *"Harada,"* came the reply. *"So you are Harada?"* (Master Egami apparently knew of him, and this, Harada thinks, is because Ohshima must have mentioned his name). The two figures alone, in the silence of the large university dojo, spoke and Egami was both impressed and interested that Harada had trained at the Shotokan. Now Harada admits: *"However hard I practised, I felt I couldn't become like Uemura or Ohshima. Something was wrong, but I didn't know what it was".*

Master Egami, who was pleased to help those who practised seriously, said that he would take him as a private student. He noted that Harada may not have the innate ability to achieve a high level of expertise, but the two of them would endeavour to find out. Egami explained that if Harada enjoyed practice but did not improve, it may be that he wasn't made for Karate, but at least he would get pleasure from finding out. On the other hand he may improve, and then there are all sorts of possibilities. The first lesson began there and then, for one hour. It was the beginning of an important friendship that lasted for many years, and which formed the basis of Master Harada's lifetime of enquiry into Karate-Do.

When Harada started training with Master Egami, some of his friends thought that he would not live to tell the tale, so fierce

*Master Egami (left) and Harada in 1954. Master Harada has stated
"Without Egami my Karate would be nothing..."*

was Egami's reputation. However, Harada persevered, and trained privately with Egami, 'person to person', for three hours a day, seven days a week, for one-and-a-half years, during 1954 and 1955. Practice was mostly conducted at the university dojo, though they would later spend many hours at Egami's house, which was situated in the Ikegami district of Tokyo, and talk about Karate, especially theory. During this time, Harada was Master Egami's only private student (though after this period he took on a further one or two from Chuo). Under Master Egami's tutorship the young Harada improved dramatically. Harada said: *"Without Egami my Karate would be nothing. My life would be completely changed."* At the dojo, Harada would practice for an hour before the lesson with his teacher, often checking his form in one of the two large mirrors in the dojo, so that his body was warmed-up. They practised until Harada's peak began to diminish. Sometimes the lesson would go on for only 30 minutes, at other times for three or four hours. Harada explained that the body is not the same each day, and you have to adapt your training accordingly. However, throughout all the time he spent with Egami, bar one exception, he practised only three techniques: *oi-zuki* (lunge punch), *gyaku-zuki* (reverse punch) and *mae-geri* (front kick). Think of the depth of enquiry into these techniques the two of them made! It is quite extraordinary. They would test the progress of the techniques on each other's abdominal muscles, protected additionally by cushions. Egami had tremendous power , Harada recalls, and would protect his student's vulnerable organs with four cushions prior to striking on the abdomen. Still the impact power of Egami's lightning techniques were sickening, to the extent that 40 years later Harada is still researching how he managed it. The notable exception mentioned above was when Harada practised 'Taikyoku Shodan' with Egami on a single occasion at a special practice held every night at Chuo University's dojo for 30 to 40 minutes.

As part of his training, Harada was once requested to attack his teacher with a right-sided *oi-zuki* in *zenkutsu-dachi* posture. On this particular occasion, Egami performed an extraordinary feat. Harada attacked with speed and Egami, without moving from the informal *hachiji-dachi* (open-leg stance), swept his right leg around in the *mikazuki-geri* (crescent kick) fashion, but instead of sweeping the inside forearm of Harada away and bringing the kick back to his chest, Egami, on touching the forearm, moved the sole of his foot over the top of the forearm, bringing it toward the wrist and applying weight. This had the effect of drawing Harada on to him and at the same time making his student bend forward, leaving his head dangerously exposed to a counter. Egami placed great value on suppleness, and this is one of the secrets of success in Karate, especially suppleness of the hip flexors. Harada demonstrated the technique slowly, openly admitting that he could not perform it. *"But Egami — he could do it. He was the only one."*

An average 1st Dan, Harada asked the famed Master Egami, who could have had his pick of the students, why he had shown an interest in him in particular. Egami replied that his soft,

Chuo University dojo, 1955, following a kyu grading. Master Harada is seated in the second row, second from the right. Master Yanagisawa is to Harada's right, followed by Masters Egami and Hironishi.

relaxed Okuyama-type style had attracted him, for that was now the focus of his own research. Certainly, the previous year (1953) Egami was astonished by the effectiveness of a new striking method he had been shown. He suddenly realised that the stiff and rigid, staccato-like movements that he had trained in for the last 25 years or so, and which were the source of a false impression, lacked true power and were seriously flawed. It was a radical new concept in striking. In the past, too much tension had been placed in the wrist, elbow and shoulder, when punching for example, and this severely restricted the release of the power in an efficient manner. The new approach had real possibilities, and Master Egami trained hard with Harada developing the method. Early in 1956, Egami had confidence in the new way of striking, but he was shortly to be struck down with illness.

On one occasion, early in 1954, Master Gogen Yamaguchi, the famous 'Cat' of the Goju-Kai, and his son came to the dojo seeking a recommendation in order that the young man might enter the university. Harada and Egami, however, paid them little attention, and were at the opposite end of the spacious dojo (formerly the Kendo dojo) intent on their own training. The nickname 'Cat', according to Yamaguchi, was given to him as a result of his perceptivity, but one fancies it may have been a result of his long hair, which quite resembled a lion's mane, although there are other possible reasons. The Master was 45 years of age at this time, and had practised Karate for 33 years, having begun under a Mr. Maruta at the Maruyama dojo on Kyushu. Four years previous to the university visit, he had formed his All-Japan Karate-Do Goju-Kai. After the war, he suffered two dreadful years in a Russian labour camp in Mongolia, but within one year of returning, had opened a dojo in Asakusa, near Ueno, Tokyo, after a religious experience. Harada recalled that father and son performed the kata 'Sanchin' together, Master Yamaguchi's shoulder-length hair, worn in the Samurai tradition, giving him the appearance of a Yamabushi (mountain warrior). An apt description, for Yamaguchi had undergone austere training on Mount Kuruma, and on Mount Ontake he would engage with his 'invisible struggle', practising takigyo (meditation under a waterfall). Master Yamaguchi became a Shinto priest and a Yoga Swami. He died on 20th May 1989, a 10th Dan.

Egami, who stood about 5ft. 6ins. tall, and at the time was in his early forties, was, as we have seen, researching and experimenting a new method of practice. This method revolved around what might best be described as a more mindful approach to Karate, based on natural movement. Harada remembers that training with Egami was physically very demanding, and when Egami blocked gedan-barai it was very strong indeed, yet when it struck one's arm, there was no pain at all. "No-one could explain this," Harada said, "Egami was different".

Harada made the point, forcefully, that he had physically experienced the effects of Egami's important research, and whereas others had later spoken to Egami about technical advancement, Harada had actually felt it during those inspired sessions, and that memory has lasted 40 years. As Master Funakoshi wrote: "What you have been taught by listening to others' words, you will forget quickly; what you have learned with your whole body you will remember for the rest of your life" ('Karate-Do, My Way Of Life', Kodansha: 1975). The result of this research was a softer, faster Karate, supposedly more powerful than the typical Shotokan practised today. Egami worked with Funakoshi until the old master died, and considered the development and direction of his research to be in line with his teacher's wishes. The author remembers reading an interview with Master Taiji Kase, 8th Dan, in which he said, intriguingly, that Egami may

Harada demonstrates a jumping-kick at the Waseda dojo in 1953.

have found something, but it was hard for his students to follow. This is almost certainly true. Egami became ill and couldn't practice, but he did pass it on — to Harada. Egami had superb *hyoshi* (timing), *choshi* (rhythm) and *ma no torikata* (distancing), but he also had something else.

Egami had been a chain-smoker and a heavy drinker of *sake*, and in 1955 was diagnosed as having severe stomach ulcers. He was operated upon twice in the space of about one year. Harada said that he never really trained again and that was another very black day indeed for the development of Karate-Do. Egami suffered at least one heart-attack in the mid-Sixties at a Summer School at Chuo University, when he had actually stopped breathing and had to be resuscitated by being given the kiss-of-life by a student and Captain of Chuo whose name was Aoki. Harada said Egami stopped breathing for some minutes, and was rushed to hospital. He was very lucky indeed, for all the necessary medical staff were on hand, and the hospital had the most up-to-date equipment. The heart-attack reduced his strength to virtually nothing. Having lost the power of speech, Egami died of a brain tumour on the 8th January 1982, leaving a wife and three sons (none of whom studied Karate, though one, Masatake, practised Aikido and Sogo-Budo).

At Harada's first university summer camp he was introduced to Master Tadao Okuyama, an outstanding 3rd Dan, and trained under him every afternoon for two years. Reading political economy, Okuyama had been Sub-Captain of Waseda University's Karate club in 1943, after the Captain had been killed in the war. He was not employed by the university, indeed he appeared to have no position, but taught and trained at his own volition. Suddenly, after a Summer Camp in 1950, Okuyama disappeared. No-one knew where he was and stories began to circulate. One of these was that apparently Master Okuyama and Master Kamata had had a disagreement over the correct method of practice, and Okuyama left, never to teach at Waseda again. In the classic tradition, the story goes, Okuyama left Tokyo alone for a life as an ascetic in the Tsukuba mountains, some 50 miles north-east of the city, to seek the true nature of Karate-Do. Harada said that *"He was very sincere — and seeking the truth"*. To survive, Okuyama would eat soup made from plants and shoot birds. For hours he would watch fish in the mountain pools and streams. Two years later he came down off the mountains with shoulder-length black hair, a shotgun across his back and a dog at his side. He wanted to travel to Hiroshima over which, of course, only seven years earlier, out of a clear blue sky the Enola Gay, from a height of five miles, parachuted the Atomic Bomb to its target. The railway authorities would not let him take his dog aboard the train, however, so he bought a pair of hiking boots and walked the 450 miles with his faithful companion beside him. Such was the character of Master Okuyama. But the story doesn't end there.

After coming down from the mountain, no-one knew, with one exception, where Okuyama lived. Many wanted to see him, but he didn't want to see them, and would not speak of his time alone. The exception was Egami, with whom he practised, and as motivation for Harada, his teacher said maybe one day, if he trained really hard and with sincerity, perhaps Okuyama would come to test him — and that day arrived one week before Harada was to leave Waseda, in April 1955. As soon as Harada

Master Egami (right), recovering from one of his bouts of illness, is visited by Master Okuyama (centre) from Kyoto, and Master Yanagisawa.

saw Master Okuyama, with his long hair and *kimono*, he said he knew he couldn't win. He could tell, just by the way he walked. *"It's impossible,"* he told Egami, *"He's too strong"*. There was something special about the man, which Harada couldn't describe. But he faced him, nonetheless. As soon as the signal was given to begin, it was over. Before Harada had taken up the *gedan-barai* position in *zenkutsu-dachi*, Okuyama was upon him. *"It was truly incredible,"* Harada recalls, *"so fast"*. Master Okuyama had attacked Harada's head with his palm. *"There was never any chance of winning."* Master Okuyama did not even touch Harada, *"But I felt the power…such power. I had never felt that before, anywhere"*. That encounter has haunted Harada all these years.

Master Okuyama was the finest and most advanced Karate-ka with whom Harada ever trained. *"He was great,"* Harada said, shaking his head, still with pale pallor, a look of shock on his face from the experience relived, in awe of a man who broke with tradition and found something. Okuyama had not been locked in the past, as many of his contemporaries had been, but was concerned with the future — how to evolve. This left him isolated, for he threatened the established norms that were in error. His livelihood was not dependent upon teaching Karate, he had nothing to protect, and so he advanced. But is it not the same today?

After the encounter Harada trained in a method that had

Master Tadao Okuyama (pictured here in 1949) was the finest and most advanced Karate-ka with whom Harada ever trained. "He was great," Harada told the author of this book, obviously still in awe of a man who broke with tradition and "found something".

been recommended to him by Master Okuyama. He hung a piece of paper up and punched at it. In the dojo, other students laughed at him, told him that he was wasting his time, and went outside to practice on the traditional form of gaining power — the makiwara. Master Okuyama had set Harada a kind of physical *koan* (a Zen riddle) and it took Harada 30 years of practice before he solved it. Initially, he could not see the value in such training, but so impressed had been by Okuyama that he dedicatedly continued. Then, one day, it suddenly dawned on him and his outlook on the nature of impact completely changed. Master Harada hasn't punched a makiwara in earnest since that time, but continues with the paper, for which he is forever in debt to Okuyama. *"He gave me a different perspective,"*

Master Okuyama teaches correct form in makiwara practice. Circa 1949.

Harada said, and this is what some of the 'old boys' at Waseda couldn't tolerate. *"Then I knew why Master Funakoshi just touched the makiwara, never pushed through. I know it looked light but there was great impact".* The author has no intention of telling the reader the value to be gained from such training, it is for the truly dedicated to discover, but he will say one thing... *"Don't push the paper, just touch it".*

Professor Mathieu (who later features prominently in this book) was told a tale by Master Harada which complements the master's experience: *"Master Dewanoumi, a Sumo chairman, once told Sensei that when he was young (about seventeen), Tochiki Yama, a very strong Yokozuna (Grand Champion), though not a big man, was explaining to them something while he was eating. It was the story of how one could throw an opponent just by grasping his belt with one's little finger. The youngsters were bored listening to this old man of 70 and most of them forgot the story. Dewanoumi was interested and did not forget. It took him three years before he could achieve his goal and so he became a Yokozuna in his turn. Had he dropped the idea, he wouldn't have succeeded. Sensei's experience with Okuyama was of the same kind and so it left its mark..."*

Okuyama had learned something whilst away, of that Harada

has little doubt — he could not be approached. A long-time training partner of Yoshitaka, Master Egami admitted to Harada that Okuyama's level was even higher than that of Yoshitaka. The level was so high, in fact, that no-one could follow him. Egami said to Harada that Okuyama was very special, but Harada already knew that...what he wanted to know was how to become special himself! *"Okuyama knew something, but he couldn't explain,"* Harada said. It was the last time he saw him. Later, when Harada returned to Japan in 1967/68 and met Egami at his house, he asked if it would be possible to see Master Okuyama. *"Maybe,"* was Egami's response, but nothing came of it. Okuyama had joined the *Omoto Kyo*, a religious sect, but never asserted his beliefs upon the students. After coming down from the mountains, he studied *Shinwa Taido* (a branch of Aikido) under Master Hoken (Noriaki) Inoue, a nephew of Morihei Ueshiba who, to say the least, appears to have been a most interesting and unorthodox character. Harada equates Master Inoue with perhaps the same ability as Master Ueshiba, the latter having taught his nephew all he knew.

Apparently Okuyama had challenged Inoue but couldn't win, so he discontinued his Karate *per se* and joined Inoue's group. Okuyama, however, was not specifically interested in Aikido, but could discern the explosive techniques within it. (Note the 'branch' of Aikido Okuyama learned was not like the Aikido one sees today.) He was not bogged down by technique, and could 'see the wood for the trees', which is actually a very rare ability. It was from Master Okuyama and the *Shinwa Taido* movement that Egami received the initial revelations with regard to his new method of practice. Egami had intended to incorporate the best aspects of his new-found learnings and apply them to Karate, but as we know, he became ill. Egami, another exceptional maverick, met similar opposition to Okuyama from at least one university and resigned.

Master Okuyama, virtually unknown in the West, is still alive and teaches *Aiki-Ken* (Aiki-sword), which he now simply calls Budo, in Kameyama, Kyoto. Master Inoue is also still teaching his art, now renamed *Shinei Taido*, to a small group of students in Kunitachi, Tokyo.

Master Harada graduated with the Bachelor of Commerce degree in 1953, and then, because of the newly-instigated American system, was able to proceed on to a Master of

Master Hoken (Noriaki) Inoue, who had a tremendous influence on both Master Okuyama and Master Egami. Inoue, now in his nineties (born 1902), still teaches in Japan. Master Harada believes him to be the finest Budoka alive today.

Commerce degree programme, awarded by assignment, under Professor Setaka. He was awarded his higher degree in 1955. Master Harada explained that master's degrees were not awarded in the old university system, where, after gaining a bachelor's degree at a sufficiently high standard, if accepted one could enrol for a further three years of study for a doctorate. However, the title of doctor was not awarded until some 10 years after completing the post-graduate course, and was based upon eminent research publications.

Whilst at the graduate school, Harada assisted Master Noguchi (another founder-member of the Waseda Karate club), who was on the faculty of the university as a lecturer in physical education (though he graduated in political economy). His style, Harada recalled, was confrontational, emphasising hard, physical contact. Harada said that he can still feel Master Noguchi's *gedan-barai!* Master Noguchi also had a position with Toshiba, and Harada would deputise for him. Notably, Harada remembered, teaching students on Wednesdays, three lessons of two hours each, which was very tiring, for one year. Master Noguchi is still alive and around 80 years of age. He created his own group, *Noguchi-Kai*, which is now run by his grandson in Kawasaki, a southern suburb of Tokyo.

Of all the famous masters of the martial arts that Harada saw in the Forties and Fifties in Japan, the outstanding Budoka, in his mind, without a shadow of a doubt was Morihei Ueshiba, the founder of Aikido. Harada tells a marvellous story of how he went with a friend to watch the diminutive, long white-bearded, literally golden-eyed Master Ueshiba at his dojo in Wakamatsu-cho, Tokyo, in late 1950 or early 1951. They walked the short, narrow path surrounded by trees and low bushes, with the composition of a Zen garden and into the all-wooden building. The friend, who had just gained his 1st Dan in Karate at Waseda, was also a black-belt in Aikido, practised hard and, partnering Ueshiba, furiously tried to strike him. The friend was thrown dramatically upon the matted floor, but the watching Harada said he couldn't see the technique — Ueshiba had not made any contact but the force of the intended technique had completely disrupted his friend's body. Harada openly admits that he was very afraid — he had never seen anything like it before. Harada's friend from that point onward completely devoted himself to Aikido, and was none other than the famous

*Mitsusuke Harada at the graduation ceremony,
Waseda University, 1953.*

Master Hiroshi Tada, 8th Dan. This master now has his own dojo in Tokyo and still teaches Aikido at Waseda.

Harada could not believe what he had seen. It troubled him greatly, and he spoke to Master Egami about what had happened. Harada remembers that a grave look came over Egami's face as he related his own encounter with Master Ueshiba, many years previously as a student, and had likewise found himself thrown without being touched. Harada distinctly remembers this conversation and the serious Egami saying: *"What you saw was true, it was real, he can do it"*. Such was the atmosphere at that meeting, and Egami's demeanour so sincere, that what Egami said next affected his student's life for the next 40 years. *"You must endeavour to produce this effect with Karate technique — this is true Karate-Do."* By Harada's own admission, this issue became, and still is, an obsession. Every day he thinks and experiments with this conclusion in mind. He believes he saw it, his much-respected teacher and friend had felt it, and it is his mission in life to discover it. As Harada said: *"After I have found it, I don't care what happens to me — my work is done"*.

What Harada had witnessed at Ueshiba's dojo in 1951 was not the outcome of being an impressionable 23-year-old under-graduate, for he saw Ueshiba's final demonstration which he gave on the 15th January 1969 in Tokyo, at the new Aikido head-quarters. Harada was 40 years old, and a man of the world. He wasn't going to be conned, but he found himself even more impressed than before — if that were possible. Ueshiba, dressed in white, and suffering from liver cancer, threw students with ease. He died three months later (26th April) aged 86. Of this final demonstration Master Harada could only use the adjective 'tremendous' to describe Ueshiba, saying that he was, without doubt, a very great man and there were no others like him. Ueshiba made it. He graduated from the dojo. There are many truly astonishing stories told of Master Ueshiba — unearthly sounds emitting from the shrine where he worshipped, an account of dematerialisation, that even though wasted away with cancer 10 students could not lift him, and so on. Whilst stories abound of martial arts masters who could supposedly do this or that, which are, quite frankly, mostly ridiculous in the extreme, being without any foundation other than through the verbal manifestations of impressionable students' imaginations, make no mistake about it, Master Harada believes in what he saw, to

Master Morihei Ueshiba, the founder of Aikido, had a deep and lasting influence upon Master Harada. To discover this Master's 'secret' became an obsession for Harada, and to this day it remains his mission in life.

Master Morihei Ueshiba evades an attack by one of his uchi-deshi (special students), Kazuo Chiba, armed with a bokken. Circa 1961.

the extent that he has based his life upon trying to emulate it.

Master Harada is still very interested in Aikido, and is great friends with the much-respected Master Kazuo Chiba, 7th Dan, who now resides in San Diego, teaching for the United States Aikido Federation. Chiba first started his martial arts career with Judo, before taking up Shotokan Karate under Master Nakayama in 1956. He later came under the influence of Morihei Ueshiba and became an *uchi-deshi*, a special student. After much exhaustive training under Ueshiba's son, Kisshomaru, Kazuo Chiba came to Britain at the request of Master Kenshiro Abbe in 1964, and Harada first met him in Birmingham that year. He stayed for 12 years before returning to Japan. Another personal friend of Harada is Master Nobuyoshi Tamura, 8th Dan, the most senior Aikidoka in Europe. Now living in Marseilles, and by all accounts an outstanding martial artist, Master Tamura practised with Ueshiba for 15 years, becoming one of his most accomplished students. He corrected Harada's *suburi* (the traditional sword-cutting motion), which Harada practises assiduously with *bokken*

A great friend of Master Harada, Kazuo Chiba is now a 7th Dan Aikido Master of world renown. He lives in San Diego, U.S.A.

of varying weights. There is possibly much to be learned from this technique, and the subject will be discussed later in this book.

In 1954 Master Harada assisted the teaching of Karate to American Air Force personnel with Masatoshi Nakayama, at the Kodokan. Shortly after this, Master Nakayama went with Master Teruyuki Okazaki to teach the Thai army and police, and at some universities in Bangkok for two months. Within the year the JKA, incorporated as an educational body under the Ministry of Education, opened its first dojo in Yotsuya, Tokyo. Originally, Ohshima had been recruited, but was unable to continue for the full three months, and half-way through Harada took over. Other famous instructors included Masters Obata, Kamata and Nishiyama. The American authorities asked the Japanese to instruct the men from the American armed forces at the beginning of the Korean War, in not only Karate, but Judo, Aikido and Kendo, as part of the USAF unarmed combat training scheme. The man responsible for this initiative was Emilio Bruno, an American Judoka of 5th Dan rank, who had trained in Japan before the war. Harada remembers that they trained every day for some 50 days, with the 15 or so students on the Judo mats, for two to three hours. Master Nakayama was at this time 41 years of age and had been practising for 22 years, having begun his training at Takushoku University under Master Funakoshi. After nine years away in China, first as a student and then working for the Chinese Government, Master Nakayama had actually taught at the American bases since 1948, with the celebrated Judo Master Kyuzo Mifune, who became a 10th Dan, and Azuo Nakayama, a Master of Kendo.

Much has been written about Masatoshi Nakayama, who became Chief Instructor to the Japan Karate Association, the world's largest Karate organisation, which at one time reportedly had ten million students worldwide. Eventually a 9th Dan, Master Nakayama considered participation in these courses to be one of the most important contributions he had made to Karate. The American SAC personnel, unlike Japanese students, constantly asked questions, and as Master Nakayama noted, under Funakoshi's guidance he began *"an intense study of kinetics, physiology, anatomy and hygienics. We believed that with a thorough grounding in the scientific basis of body mechanics, we would find it easier to teach foreigners. We were right, and we also learned a great deal about our own practise of the art"* ('Conversations With The Master: Masatoshi Nakayama', R. G. Hassell, Focus: 1983).

The airforce men went back to America and to NATO countries and began teaching Karate. This formed the basis for the subsequent tremendous interest in the art. The courses also provided the seed for Nakayama's famous technical guide to Shotokan, 'Karate-Do Shinkyotei' (*A New Method of Teaching Karate-Do*) which, in abridged form, became 'Dynamic Karate', published in 1966. Harada described Master Nakayama as an excellent instructor and first-rate demonstrator, having very good adaptation with beautiful timing. Harada classed him as a Type 3 personality (along with Gichin Funakoshi) — one characterised by orderliness, preciseness and efficiency of technique. An instructor rather than a fighter, it was partly Master Nakayama's 'personality type', Harada said, that motivated and allowed the type of impressive JKA expansion worldwide. (Note that no

*Master Harada and Master Ohshima outside the main entrance to the
Waseda University dojo, 1953, with two members of the United States
Air Force special training personnel.*

The former Chief Instructor of the Japan Karate Association, Master Masatoshi Nakayama (1913-1987). In 1954, Harada and Nakayama both assisted with the teaching of Karate to American Air Force personnel at the Kodokan Judo dojo. Master Harada described his colleague as "An excellent instructor and first-rate demonstrator..."

ranking is implied in these 'personality types', and the numbers 1, 2 and 3 are at the nominal level of measurement.) The two of them would instruct the servicemen in self-defence and a little 'Heian' kata practice. The pay was good, Harada recalls, and he enjoyed the experience. Master Nakayama died of a stroke on the 15th April 1987.

Harada recalled: *"When he* (Nakayama) *started competition, I was very surprised because originally he really didn't want competition"*. At Waseda, the university students experimented with competition under Ohshima, and later provided a special free-style display. Master Nakayama attended and he *"really, really complained to me: 'Why do you do it?'"* Harada said that Nakayama was at the time (1952), *"very strongly against it"*. I wonder, why did he change?

3

Karate
Goes To
South
America

Mitsusuke Harada continued the pioneering work of Master Funakoshi when, in 1955, he introduced Karate-Do to South America. He is shown here midway through his favourite kata 'Enpi'.

The journey of 18 miles south from Tokyo to the major seaport on the east coast of Honshu, Yokohama, sited on the west shore of Tokyo Bay, was a busy one. Standing on a plain shut in by hills, Yokohama harbour, although somewhat exposed, was spacious and, of course, convenient. It had been a small fishing village only 100 years previously, but now Japan's principal port was rapidly growing with a population well over one million in 1955, double that of 1935, exporting silks and tea to the West. The city had been almost completely destroyed by fire, and a vast number of its population killed in the Great Kanto Earthquake of 1923. It was from here, early in 1955, that Master Harada set sail for Brazil aboard the *Africa Maru*.

Master Egami, whom Harada had trained under the night before, Master Motohiro Yanagisawa (a physical education lecturer at Chuo University and a student of Egami) and his son, Daisuke, saw Harada off. His parents and sister agreed with his going to Brazil and had, on their son's wishes, said their farewells previously. Harada's mother particularly wanted to see her son off, but he had opposed this for he felt that things would get too emotional for all concerned, and didn't want any tears. Harada had never intended living in Japan, and certainly had no regrets about leaving. He was delighted when he was offered the post abroad, to work in a bank. Being born and raised in Manchuria, not exposed to the regimented, unquestioning and rigid formality in his formative years so typical of pre-war Japan, Harada found it difficult to fit in. He was uncomfortable, a square peg in a round hole. His father was also very encouraging, remembering his own inhibited upbringing. "*Whatever you want to do, you must do it*," he told his son.

The sea voyage, a trip of some 13,500 nautical miles, across the Pacific to Los Angeles, skirting the coast of Mexico and Central America, through the Panama Canal into the Caribbean, entering the Atlantic, passing through the Equator and on to Rio de Janeiro, took 40 days. It began badly, with everyone on board being seasick for the first four or five days. Due to the high seas, the Captain sailed further south and into calmer weather and health was restored aboard. The stop-off at Los Angeles, their first port-of-call, was initially for one day, but due to a cargo handlers' strike, the ship was docked for a week. Master Ohshima met Harada from the boat, having been in California only a very short while, and they spent an enjoyable week sightseeing.

Tsutomu Ohshima is generally recognised (other than returning US military personnel) as the man who introduced traditional Karate to North America. He opened the first-ever Karate dojo in 1956, in Los Angeles, California and that same year formed the South California Karate Association. Today, Master Ohshima's organisation, Shotokan Karate of America, has over 140 dojos in the U.S. and Canada, and affiliations world-wide.

During the long, hot days, Harada used to practice kata on the deck of the ship. Passengers on board were almost exclusively Japanese immigrant agricultural workers. Japan had an official immigration policy to Brazil. Some 200,000 settled in the first half of this century along the east coast of Brazil, between Rio de Janeiro and Sao Paulo, showing great cohesion as rural settlers. Other notable immigrants were Italians, Portuguese, Spaniards, Germans and Eastern Europeans. Master Harada recalled that these Japanese were very interested in Karate, and he used to teach them kata on deck.

As the *Africa Maru* came close to Rio, far away, south-west, beyond the city limits, stood Gavea, an isolated, flat-topped rock over 2,300ft. in height, resembling a reclining giant. As the Captain steered his ship in water known for its dangerous swells and into the entrance of the beautiful natural harbour, a mile wide, between the Sugar Loaf Mountain, a conical rock rising 1,300ft. above water level on the west side and the Parrot's Beak on the east, with forts on either side, Harada knew that his journey was near to ending.

Upon entering Guanabara Bay, the flourishing port's foundries, mills, refineries, breweries, shipyards and railway works came into view. Beyond, the many fine buildings, and further still the Sera da Carioca Mountains to the south and most notably Corcovado, a sharp, rocky peak 2,300ft. in height with the imposing statue, 100ft. high, of Christ the Redeemer. To the north, the wooded heights of the Serra do Mar. Along the quays were ships laden with sugar, cotton, tobacco, rubber, meat, hides, timber, thorium, diamonds, and particularly coffee. This was a bustling port and city of over three million people and it was growing fast.

They docked in Rio for one day while immigration formalities were satisfied and then Harada continued by ship to the world's chief coffee port, Santos, some 250 miles south-west of Rio. He was then met by a car sent from the bank and driven the 30 miles

Master Tsutomu Ohshima... the man responsible for introducing traditional Karate to North America.

Harada working at the Bank of South America, Sao Paulo, 1958.

to his final destination, Sao Paulo. The largest industrialised centre of the nation, Sao Paulo was nicknamed the 'Chicago of South America'. With a population of three million, it had its attractively-laid-out residential areas, but these contrasted sharply with the industrial slums. But generally it was an agreeable city in 1955, with a cathedral and monasteries. Despite its

Pre-arranged sparring practice in the first Karate club in South America.

importance, however, Sao Paulo was appreciably smaller than the mid-Fifties Tokyo that Harada was familiar with, having only a third as many people. Situated on the Tropic of Capricorn, on a high plateau some 2,400ft. in height, Sao Paulo was sited in a healthy location on the River Tiete. Like Rio, it was a fast-growing commercial and industrial centre, with characteristic skyscrapers, trebling its population in the 20 years from 1935 and subsequently trebling it again in the next 25 years to become today the leading city in South America. In 1955, as Harada looked about him, he saw flour mills, breweries, distilleries, the production of textiles, clothing, boots and shoes, glass, chemicals, cottons, woollens and furniture. The rich red soil of the hinter-land produced huge supplies of sugar-cane, cereals, fruit, tobacco, but once again especially coffee. Indeed, the Sao Paulo area was, and still is, the chief coffee-growing area in the world.

Harada took up his position at the Bank of South America, sit-uated in the Rua Senadorjo, in the centre of the city opposite a University of Sao Paulo faculty site, working in the foreign exchange and credit markets. It was well-paid and he finally worked his way up to chief cashier, which carried with it a very good salary. He lived for the first two years lodging with an

A Karate demonstration in the University of Sao Paulo in 1958.
Master Harada has his back to the camera.

Italian family of nine. They were office workers too and Harada
very much enjoyed his stay, noting how friendly his landlord was.
Later he took out a favourable loan with his bank and bought an
attractive apartment on the sixth floor of a small ten-storey
block. The difference in the standard of living between post-war
Tokyo and mid-Fifties Sao Paulo was, according to Harada, like
comparing black with white. He had a marvellous stay in
the city.

Harada had been told, prior to leaving Tokyo, that there were
already JKA instructors in Brazil. In fact this was incorrect information and no-one was teaching Karate there. For the first six
months Harada trained by himself, informally, and had no defi-
nite plans to start teaching. The manager of the bank, learning of
Harada's Karate expertise, asked whether he would be prepared
to give a demonstration for the staff. Harada said that he would
be pleased to oblige and was told to take the company car to collect his *gi*. After the demonstration, one person came to him and
asked whether he could be taken on as a student. Harada said
that this might be possible, but unfortunately he had nowhere to
practice. The young man was insistent and said that he would
find somewhere. Time passed and Harada had almost forgotten

A demonstration at a military establishment in 1959, given by Master Harada and his students.

about the agreement, when the budding student said he had found a Judo dojo which they could use.

They began training together in October 1955. A short while later the student's nephew began training with them and then other members of their family, accompanied by interested friends. Harada did not advertise the art he was teaching. His few students belonged to the Japanese community, and not long afterwards the local Japanese magazine heard of the training and came along to the dojo for an interview with Harada and to take some photographs. When published, this produced the first influx of 'outside' Japanese students. Later, *La Gazetta de Sport*, a Brazilian sports magazine, also came for an interview, and as a consequence of the article that appeared, Brazilians started to train as well. In fact the club grew in numbers to some 30 to 40 students and Karate-ka outnumbered their host's Judo students. Apparently this did provoke a little jealousy in the local

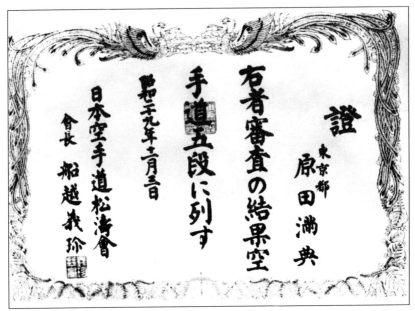

Master Harada's 5th Dan certificate — signed by Gichin Funakoshi.

***Certification of Harada as a Professor of Karate — signed by
Shigeru Egami.***

Judo world, but on the whole they got on very well together. Harada also had contact with the Chinese community, for he was interested in Tai Chi, but the Chinese did not really want to mix, and kept themselves very much to themselves.

In the evenings then, after a full day's work, Harada taught Karate three or four nights a week. Banking hours were between mid-day and 4 p.m., but Harada had to be at the office at 9 a.m. or often 8 a.m., and generally stayed until 5 p.m. Sometimes, however, especially when they were expecting important correspondence from Tokyo, he could be there until midnight. He worked Monday to Friday and Saturday mornings. On Sunday he rested.

The club he founded, the first Karate club not only in Brazil, but in the whole of South America, was located just two minutes' walk from the bank, and was therefore very convenient. The club was, in fact, at the dojo of Master Hikari Kurachi, a famous Pan-American Judo champion, then ranked 5th or 6th Dan. The dojo was situated on the third or fourth floor, was matted, had white painted walls and a low ceiling. At one end there were large, patio-like windows, which opened out on to a narrow balcony. In fact, Karate had become a noticeable novelty, and Master Harada appeared on television twice, once in Sao Paulo (1956) and once in Rio (1957), performing pre-arranged sparring on a short slot for Brazilian viewers. The Physical Education Department of the University of Brazil, in Rio, contacted him for they too were interested in Karate. He obtained special permission from the bank, and was permitted to demonstrate for a week in 1957. This was one of many displays he and his students gave in the late Fifties.

Training at the dojo was between 7.30 p.m. and 9.30 p.m., but as they were naturally guests of the Judoka, they had to fit in with their practice, so often it would be 8.30 to 10.00. Master Harada wanted to affiliate his club with Japan and wrote to Master Funakoshi expressing this wish, but Funakoshi replied firmly stating that he should start up a Brazilian organisation, which he duly did. Harada said that he was "*Very shocked by O'Sensei's response, but at the same time very pleased and encouraged*". You see, Funakoshi had brought to the Japanese mainland an Okinawan art which he believed to have great individual and social value. However, matters had not turned out quite as the old master had wished, and he considered the art to have been

Master Harada poses with a group of his students in Brazil,
in September 1957.

largely spoiled and corrupted. Harada is certain that Funakoshi
hoped to avoid the general decline in the spiritual and moral values, the squabbling and bureaucratic mess that Japanese Karate
had found itself in, by allowing Brazilian Karate to start afresh
under Harada, who, of course, Funakoshi knew particularly well.
And so, Karate-Do Shotokan Brazileo was born.

It was at this time, as an endorsement of Funakoshi's belief in
him that, at the very young age of 28, Harada received his 5th
Dan from Master Funakoshi. Harada explained that he did not
have the opportunity to grade to 2nd Dan and beyond whilst in
Japan, and Master Funakoshi was obviously aware of this.Harada
first wrote to Master Egami requesting a more senior grade, as 1st
Dan was an insufficient rank for the Japanese community (especially the Okinawans) in Brazil, and gave up teaching for a few
months. Egami, fully appreciative of the situation, replied that he
would recommend a 3rd Dan. This was not a sufficient grade for
Harada to continue, however, and he wrote back requesting that
Egami ask Master Funakoshi (Funakoshi was too old to write to
directly given the immediacy of the situation), and Egami sent
the signed, back-dated (3rd of November, 1954) 5th Dan
certificate to Brazil.

Master Gichin Funakoshi's Memorial stands in the grounds of the Zen Temple of Engaku-ji in Kamakura. It bears his words "Karate ni sente nashi" ("There is no first attack in Karate").

Master Harada has never sought a Dan rank beyond *Godan*, explaining that such grades are meaningless really. Masters Ohshima and Hironishi never graded beyond *Godan*, and Egami not beyond *Yondan* (in fact, Master Egami actually refused a 5th Dan from the JKA, an association he had little time for). The Shotokai do not award grades beyond 5th Dan, and who would grade such masters anyway? Only a group of seniors and they would be bound by group decision, and on that basis the award would have little value. In the West, most Shotokan associations customarily work on a minimum of two years from 1st Dan to 2nd Dan, a further minimum three years from 2nd Dan to 3rd Dan, a further minimum four years from 3rd Dan to 4th Dan, and so on. It is interesting to note, therefore, that as Master Harada was awarded his 5th Dan in 1956, using the above as a comparative method, he would be a 9th Dan today and in line for 10th Dan in 1996 — if such a thing were desirable. The author believes the projection to be a valid one. It is a sobering thought that Harada was a Master of Karate many years before some very famous practitioners, themselves now masters of repute, even started training.

In late April 1957, Harada received a telegram from Master Egami informing him that Master Funakoshi had passed away quietly in hospital on the 26th of that month.Egami had actually been at his old teacher's bedside when the Master took his last breath, along with members of the family. Harada said that Funakoshi's last years were not happy ones. He had become isolated, disenchanted, very lonely and used, and although a little senile, quietly he felt deep despair. Harada felt the old master had nothing to live for. He did not have any disciples, as Ueshiba had, who would take care of him, and Harada felt that this was a great pity, describing the situation as *"really tragic"*. Egami had taken on the role of looking after the old master and had learned much from him, but when Egami fell ill (Harada was informed of Egami's stomach operation by Master Yanagisawa), and could no longer fulfill his duties, no-one took his place. The author asked Master Harada how he had felt when he received the news of his teacher's death. *"I did not feel sad. He had had a long and worthwhile life,"* was the reply.

Funakoshi's family objected to a particularly well-known association, and one bureaucrat of that organisation in particular (whose name does not appear in this book and who Funakoshi apparently genuinely disliked) arranging the funeral. There were a number of reasons for this, but once again the author is not at liberty to say why. Suffice it to say that the family, Yoshihide in particular, felt very strongly. A group had to be formed to attend to the funeral, and the name Shotokai was chosen with Yoshihide (who did not practise Karate) as the first Chairman. Yoshihide died only some four years after his father. At this stage the name 'Shotokai' had no Karate significance, other than that the family deemed that the senior grades who were asked to participate had a close connection with the Funakoshi family. Such members were Masters Hironishi, Egami and Yanagisawa. Members of this group were executors to the estate, and thus trusted by the family. Under the direction of Dr. Nobumoto Ohama, an Okinawan, who was a professor of commercial law as well as the President of Waseda University, and a personal friend of the Funakoshi family, Waseda joined. Other influential members of the university, however, did not want to get involved and wanted to follow Keio, so Waseda immediately left the group after the funeral, as did a number of other universities.

After the funeral, the Shotokai was not dissolved and the universities that remained were Chuo, Senshu, Toho, Gakushuin and Tokyo Noko (an agricultural university). It was not a question of technique at this stage, all were practising the same Shotokan method. Master Egami wrote to Master Harada to inform him of the state of affairs and subsequent developments. Harada, with his close association with Masters Funakoshi and Egami, followed Egami and became a member of the Shotokai.

The sad state of affairs surrounding Funakoshi's funeral disappointed Yutaka Harada greatly. He wrote to his son saying how very surprised and disappointed he was that all of Funakoshi's students couldn't even come together at their teacher's farewell. But let us be positive. We shall say that Funakoshi's students could not agree in which direction the founder's style should develop. It may be argued that the Shotokai were dedicated to preserving the orthodox teachings of Funakoshi, and Egami believed that future development was along the path that the old master had intended. Certainly one may make an assumption and say that Funakoshi did not approve completely of the direction in which certain senior Karate-ka were taking the art.

In June 1958, special celebrations were held to mark the sixtieth anniversary of Japanese business in Brazil. The Brazilian Government invited a number of Japanese dignitaries, and chief among these were Prince Mikasa (Emperor Hirohito's youngest

Harada acting as a Royal bodyguard in Sao Paulo, June 1958.

brother) and his wife, the Princess Yuriko. There was much worry, for the Japanese surrender in the Pacific War thirteen years earlier was still a moot question to many a dissatisfied patriot. There was concern that an attempt on the life of the Prince and Princess might be made. Matters were complicated because Sao Paulo was hosting an important football match between Brazil and Sweden at the same time and there was a large influx of fans. It was decided that the couple would be protected by Japanese bodyguards, for it was deemed undiplomatic that, should a problem arise, Brazilian bodyguards would be seen fighting off Japanese dissidents. Three senior Judoka were chosen: Professor Kihara, 7th Dan; Professor Katayama, 6th Dan; and Mr. Fukaya, 4th Dan. The director of Harada's bank, Mr. Kunoto Mysaka, suggested that, because Harada practised Karate, he might offer his services, despite it being a particularly hectic time at the bank. Mr. Mysaka was very impressed by Harada's Karate and greatly encouraged this 'other side' in his employee's character. Harada was, at first, reluctant to take the job, but the Japanese Consul personally asked him to, so he succumbed, and for two weeks protected the Princess and the State Governor's wife along with Professor Katayama. Harada said that he thoroughly enjoyed himself, travelling in a special aircraft of the Brazilian President, and so on. At night he retired to his apartment and the Royal couple stayed, protected, in the State Governor's residence. The Royal party, who were pursued continually by the media, including Japanese journalists who had come from Japan specifically to cover the events, toured the States of Sao Paulo and Parana before flying to Peru, where the Prince was able to study the remains of the Incas (Prince Makasa became a professor of archaeology in Tokyo).

For security, it had been decided to split the Royal party into two. Harada always accompanied the second black limousine. Master Harada remembers the procession of cars passing along the Rua Senadorjo, and the director of the bank bowed low as the Royal party and bodyguards went past. Harada was very embarrassed by this, for he said he felt as though the director was bowing to him. For this potentially very dangerous work, Harada got paid precisely nothing! As he said, he was just a body to stand in front of the Princess should anything happen — to allow some small time for escape action to take place. Prince Mikasa did, however, give him a silver cigarette case as a token gesture

Master Harada strengthens his uraken (back-fist) on the makiwara.

(Harada, who does not smoke, later gave this to Hiromu Ishihara, a fellow-Shotokai Karate-ka and friend, who teaches in Hiroshima). Harada liked the Prince, but was very surprised at his frank language. Apparently Prince Mikasa had been a Major in the army, where he had learned the niceties of the more vulgar tongue! In contrast, the Princess was very aloof.

Also in 1958, the famous Rikidozan, an ex-*Sumotori* turned

professional wrestler, came to Sao Paulo and was introduced to Harada by a close friend. Rikidozan — real name Mitsuharu Momota — attained the rank of *Sekiwake*, two grades below *Yokozuna* (Grand Champion) before quitting Sumo in 1950 to introduce Western-style Pro-wrestling to Japan. After becoming rich and famous from this venture, he died tragically, in 1963, aged 39, the victim of a knife attack in a Tokyo nightclub.

Another incident that Master Harada recalls during his stay in Brazil was when Eder Jofre came to the dojo with his manager. Jofre, who was born in Sao Paulo in 1936, was a boxer of the first order, regarded by many as the best in the world for nearly 20 years. Standing just 5ft. 4ins. in height, this little Brazilian had a superb physique, and was devastating with both hands. He was noted particularly for a lightning jab and a tremendous hook. His first professional fight had been held on his 21st birthday, and he was one of only two world champion boxers to have been a vegetarian (the result of his father having taken him to a slaughter-house as a child). He took the vacant Bantamweight title on the 18th of November 1960, by knocking-out Eloy Sanchez in Round 6 in a fight staged in Los Angeles. He held the title for four-and-a-half years, beating eight further contenders, with his first defence staged in Rio against Piero Rollo of Italy, and his third and fifth defence in Sao Paulo against Johnny Caldwell of Great Britain and Joe Medel of Mexico, respectively.

Jofre had heard of a famous 'Fighting Harada', and thought that Mitsusuke might be the brother of this famed fighter, and had come to investigate, though of course, it was a case of mistaken identity. The two men talked about boxing and Karate, though because Master Harada spoke no Portuguese and Jofre no Japanese, they had to go through an interpreter. Harada recalled, however, that the manager did most of the talking, and Jofre was generally very quiet. Jofre stayed for about 30 minutes and Master Harada liked him a great deal. Jofre wasn't interested in the kicking techniques of Karate at all, just the punches. Jofre put a light glove on and punched at Harada's opened hand. Master Harada was impressed by his strength and speed, and the flowing way in which he moved. Jofre then let Harada place his fist upon his abdominal muscles and release *kime* (focus of vital spirit). Jofre was apparently surprised at the strength of the explosive power of the technique. The boxer's body movements gave Master Harada the distinct feeling that Karate was too

*Master Harada palms away a determined mae-geri (front kick), and is
about to counter with a punch to the head.*

static. This was Jofre's first encounter with Karate, and Harada
said that each confessed to one another that they were wary. It
was, in fact, 'Fighting Harada' who ended Jofre's reign at a title
fight in Nagoya, on points, after fifteen rounds. A little over a
year later, Jofre attempted to regain the title in Tokyo, but again
the decision went against him. 'Fighting Harada' was the only
man ever to beat Jofre. He retired and then made a spectacular
comeback, by taking the World Featherweight title in Brazilia on
points against Jose Legra of Cuba, and then knocked-out
Vincente Saldivar of Mexico in Round 4 five months later. He
forfeited WBC recognition for failing to defend his title against
Alfredo Marcano, and retired in 1976, with a record of 78 fights,
72 wins, four draws and two defeats.

Another story around this time involved a supposed friend of
Harada bringing to the dojo a senior practitioner of the Brazilian
fighting art of Capoeira. Capoeira grew out of the culture of the
African slaves transported to Brazil at the end of the 18th
Century. Because the hands of the slaves were invariably mana-
cled, the wide use of the legs and feet, with many spinning and
sweeping techniques, were devised. Capoeira was practised as an
energetic, aerobatic, free expressive dance accompanied by
music, but the truth was that such movements hid a more

Pioneering Karate — on the back streets of Sao Paulo.

deadly purpose. Secretly, this 'friend' had brought the Capoeira specialist to challenge Master Harada. Harada did not know this and the 'friend' gave no indication as to his intention. However, another student, who could speak Portuguese and Japanese, overheard their conversation and told Harada what was planned. Master Harada, now fully aware of what was going on, stepped up the intensity of dojo training, working himself and his students really hard, with the Capoeirista looking on from the side of the dojo. At the end of the lesson Harada applied a little more psychology and approached the Capoeirista before he could offer his challenge. Harada said he would accept a challenge any time one was offered, but the professor of Capoeira declined the offer and never visited the dojo again.

On another occasion, however, at the University of Brazil dojo in Rio de Janeiro, a challenge by a Capoeira master was offered and Harada accepted. Remember, these were pioneering days. The two men faced each other, and the Capoeirista entered the *jogo* ('game') and started to move speedily with the rhythm of the accompanying music played on the *berimbau*, a single-string bow with a sound box made from a gourd, the *pandeiro* (tambourine) and *atabaque* (native drum). Harada explained that the man breathed to the tempo of the music and, catching the breathing, each time the man took an inhilation, Harada advanced and drove him into a corner. He then clearly showed a technique that would have ended matters, but did not go

Gyaku-zuki (reverse punch) practice on the makiwara.

through with it, so that the man did not lose face. Master Harada said that the Capoeira he had encountered was the real thing — very dangerous and very good, and he had been lucky.

One encounter with a Capoeirista could have had unforeseen consequences, had Master Harada not taken his own sound

Master Harada demonstrates kumite (sparring) in 1957.

advice of never making unnecessary enemies. Harada had beaten the Capoeirista, but had not humiliated him in public. The gentleman concerned, as it turned out, was a high-ranking member of the local underworld. Harada recalls that even the shoeshine boy would not allow him to pay when he had his shoes cleaned in the city streets!

Harada kept in regular touch with Master Egami. The two would correspond by letter. Harada would send photographs of himself and his students and ask his teacher's opinion. This correspondence lasted for three or four years. Master Egami actually hated writing letters, but later considered all their correspondence to be of sufficient merit that a book could have been based upon them. Unfortunately, they were left behind in Sao Paulo when Harada later moved to Europe. Master Harada very much regrets this, as I am sure all readers do. Harada gave them to a friend for safe-keeping, but this friend went back to Japan, and passed them on to another friend who lost them.

After the problems encountered in business, Master Egami found it difficult, in post-war Japan, to 'make ends meet'. With the onset of his ulcers and the subsequent operations, his financial situation was dire. Because airmail postage was quite expensive, Harada's father paid the cost of Egami's replies to his son's letters. Egami had real difficulty making a living. As he wrote: *"I look back at this time, during which I was plunged into abject*

Correcting a student's form. Photo circa 1957.

despair, as the worst period of my life" ('*The Heart of Karate-Do'*, Kodansha: 1980).

It was during this time, whilst Harada was in Brazil, that an unfortunate incident occurred back in Tokyo that forever soured their relationship. Master Harada did not wish the author to include details of this episode in the book, and honour-bound, I shall not. There are, in any case, two sides to any story, and Master Egami is unable to tell his account. However, from that point onward the Harada family, especially his mother and sister, whilst appreciative of the value of Karate-Do, were not-so-well disposed to a certain Karate-ka. This opposition had a very deep, profound, upsetting and lasting impact on Harada, and provides one probable basis as to why, given the reaction of his mother and sister to the incident (which, by Western standards, might be judged as personal yet quite minor), he never married. Master Harada, to this day, does not initiate discussion on Karate with his family, and his mother and sister never enquire.

Master Harada did have a number of girl-friends when living in Sao Paulo. One, an attractive Brazilian named Marta, lived with him in his apartment for three months before they parted. Harada tells an amusing, if irresponsible story associated with his time with Marta. He had a photograph of them together and, as a joke, sent it to his family in Tokyo informing them that he had got married. His father was very surprised, congratulated them, and sent Marta a pearl necklace. Master Harada, realising that the joke had backfired, wrote to Egami and asked him to explain to his parents. Egami wrote back in an understandably angry mood, not very impressed with Harada's sense of humour. *"What,"* the author asked, *"became of the pearl necklace?"* Master Harada, laughing, explained that he gave it to his next girl-friend!

Master Egami's wife, Chiyoko, wrote: *"Although Mr. Harada came back to Japan once and then parted with awkwardness, he is still my husband's junior whom he is always anxious about,"* and *"Even when my husband was dying he was anxious about Mr. Harada"* (from a translation of a newsletter of the Fujitsu Company Karate Club). But Harada had been deeply offended. Filled with unease, he felt that the proprieties had not been observed... but what a shame. The two of them still corresponded on a monthly basis however, until the late Seventies.

There were other forces at work too, intervening in their relationship. When Master Egami and his wife came to France in 1976 through an invitation by Master Tetsugi Murakami, they were under the impression that Master Harada did not want to see them. In truth, nothing could have been further from Master Harada's mind. As Professor Bernard Mathieu (who makes a significant contribution to the next chapter) recalls: *"I can testify that I was there when Harada Sensei tried to convince Mr. Murakami that they should join forces so as to provide a proper welcome for Egami — a dialogue which lasted for twelve hours in Paris. Will I ever forget it! Just think that later the same character managed to 'exclude' Harada Sensei when Egami visited Europe, thus getting all the publicity it brought for himself."* The author believes that this unfortunate state of affairs operated in at least one other country, with one other instructor.

After that acrimonious meeting, the relationship between Murakami and Harada finished. They had no further communication with one another. Similarly, when Master Egami came to London, Harada couldn't see him because he had found out about the visit too late and had a special weekend course in Scotland that he was committed to attending. Master Egami did not teach on a course in England. Master Harada said because of ill-health Egami did not want to show technique. Whilst quite

Master Harada with Master Ohshima during their 1959/60 get-together.

understandable, Harada believed that, as Chief Instructor to the Shotokai, he should have done something. Although a division was now between them, Harada said that he has very fond memories of Master Egami, and wants to remember him as a tremendous influence not only upon his technique, but upon his life in general.

In late December 1959, Master Ohshima, now a 5th Dan, awarded from Waseda University, came to stay and train with Harada and his students. Ohshima, as usual, was keen, orthodox and very good. The fact that Master Harada had been awarded his 5th Dan from Funakoshi was apparently the subject of some joking and friendly banter. Ohshima's one-off trip lasted for two weeks and into the New Year, and they had a very good time together. They met up with Master Masahiko Kimura, a famous Judoka and Professor of Judo at Takushoku University, who had come to Brazil to teach for a short period. It is worth noting that Master Kimura had known, and had great respect for, Master Morihana, the famous Shotokan kick specialist. In fact, Harada believes the two men had been in the army together and may have had a friendly contest, which Morihana won with a kick.

At the time Master Harada was not charging his students for training, but Ohshima advised him to do so, otherwise his Karate

Master Harada demonstrates a block and simultaneous kekomi (thrust kick) counter.

would not be respected. It is a curious fact that what you do not pay for in the West is generally regarded as not worth anything because it is free, whereas in contrast, in Japan, free instruction has greater value because there is feeling and personal involvement. It is interesting to note, therefore, that when Master Harada thereafter charged for his instruction, he actually had more students attend. Crazy it may be, but true, the two cultures having a different set of values.

By 1963, Master Harada had a regular attendance at his dojo of about 20 to 25 students. He had graded some 16 or 17 to 1st Dan in all, though some of these had left. The first pupil to be graded to black-belt was a Mr. Yasuda, a fellow-bank employee, born of Japanese parents but holding Brazilian nationality. No-one had yet attained 2nd Dan. Other Karate instructors were beginning to come to Brazil, and the usual petty rivalries began to rear their ugly head. If the opportunity arose, it was time for a change. Time to move on.

4

An Invitation
To Europe

Master Harada pictured in Brussels, October 1963.

A French student, Oliver Perois, training with Harada in Sao Paulo, returned to France and visited a small number of dojos in Paris. One of these was run by a Vietnamese named Hoang Nam, now dead, whose own Karate background seems to be of uncertain origin. Perois was apparently unimpressed at the level of expertise, and gave his opinion to the students, who were very surprised. Perois told them about Master Harada, and they raised sufficient funds to buy an air ticket so that Harada could visit them in Europe. Hoang Nam, whom Harada described as being very small in height, about 5ft. *"physically very clever, but would not do kumite,"* was apparently not-too-happy about this arrangement.

Having learned of the offer Master Harada had received, the manager of the bank encouraged his subordinate to go to Europe, explaining that it was an opportunity not to be missed, and that he would suspend his position for one year, so that he could take up his old duties when he returned. However, another clique within the bank opposed Master Harada's plans and the effect of this was that, in December 1962, he resigned from the bank and sold his apartment. The manager, however, took Harada to one side and said that when he returned a job would be waiting for him and he need not fear. In fact, of course, Master Harada never returned to the banking profession; had he done so, there is little doubt that, with the fullness of time, he would have occupied a senior position somewhere in the world. However, without a wife and children, Harada said, it would have been slow progress, for such conventions were expected in the banking world. He never regretted leaving the bank, though. The atmosphere was stifling, and there was *"no room for personal creation"*, as Harada put it. He explained that many people were trying for promotion, there were dirty games being played, and he simply found it difficult to concentrate on such things.

Harada has never really had any money and never sought it. His philosophy is: *"Just enough — that is all,"* and he pursued his Karate-Do in a pure way. He had always been painfully aware that if he had married and had had a family, his Karate might have suffered. *"It could have been good, if the wife agreed. But what if things changed and she didn't agree?"* Making a living from Karate and supporting a family was always far too precarious for him. He might have had to compromise and lower his standards. Additionally, he would have had to travel and be away from home a great deal, which, of course, is not conducive to family life. He said that a friend of his, of exceptional Karate ability, had married and been very happy, his wife having shared her husband's interest. When she died, however, he gave up training.

Harada did return to Sao Paulo in 1979, to visit his bank friends and pupils, for a month's holiday. A series of articles appeared in the Brazilian press, where he was described as the original importer of Karate to Brazil. Although more than 30 years has elapsed, Master Harada still regularly corresponds with three friends from his days in Sao Paulo. Shinchi Aiba and Fugio Tachebana still live in Brazil. Yoshiharu Matsumoto returned to Japan after one year, but still sends Master Harada a monthly magazine and also any books that Harada requests. All three friends reached very senior positions in the business world. (One of Master Harada's wishes is to take a world cruise and visit his old friends in Sao Paulo again.)

In February 1963, Master Harada's plane touched down in Paris, and he planned to stay for no more than one year. The Brazilian dojo was, meanwhile, in the capable hands of one of his students, awaiting his return. This invitation co-incided with an additional call for Harada to come to France to take over from Master Ohshima.

Another instructor with his base in Paris at this time was Tetsugi Murakami, who had a dojo in the Rue Cambronne. The lithe, moustached, 30-year-old Yoseikan 3rd Dan, Murakami had come to France in November 1957 at the invitation of Henri Plee, the 'Funakoshi of Europe', under a one-year contract, but had remained, having built up a following. He had managed to stay in France by joining the *Alliance Francaise* language course. Murakami had apparently been a student of a certain Masaji Yamaguchi in Shizuoka, having started training in 1946, before practising at the JKA. He had also studied Aikido under the famed Master Minoru Mochizuki.

Harada had not heard of Murakami before coming to France, and in fact said that no-one he knew in Japan had known him either. Murakami told Harada that he had trained in Goju under Master Gogen Yamaguchi, but Harada noted that Murakami didn't know the kata 'Sanchin' or 'Tensho', which seemed strange as these are fundamental forms in the Goju system. Harada believes that Murakami attended the JKA in 1957, probably as a pupil of Masters Hidetaka Nishiyama and/or Teruyuki Okazaki,

Master Tetsugi Murakami (1927-1987) was the first Japanese Karate sensei to teach the art in Gt. Britain; this was in 1959.

but only for a very short period, perhaps some two months. It does seem rather strange that when officials in Italy requested some kind of certificate or testimony to show that Murakami was a bona fide instructor, he had to ask Harada to get Master Egami to furnish him with such evidence, a 5th Dan, which Harada did.

Murakami was the first Japanese Karate instructor to teach in Great Britain, being invited to do so by Vernon Bell and the

This historic photo (circa 1960) shows Master Murakami leading a group of British Karate-ka in kihon waza (basic techniques).

British Karate Federation in 1959, and was by all accounts impressive, providing a high spot for the early trainees. A very strict and uncompromising teacher, he taught the 'Heian' katas and pre-arranged sparring. Murakami visited G.B. fairly regularly between 1959 and 1964. In 1967 he returned briefly to Japan, and came under the influence of Master Egami's Shotokai (though Harada says that he never practised with Egami). He formed his own association and had students in a number of European and African countries, including Algeria, Angola, Belgium, Italy, Morocco, Portugal and Switzerland. He died of cancer on the 24th of January 1987.

It is believed that the first Japanese Karate-ka to teach formally in Europe was Hiroo Mochizuki, the son of Minoru Mochizuki. He first came to Paris in 1957, a Yoseikan 2nd Dan. Returning to Japan before journeying back to France to study veterinary medicine, Hiroo Mochizuki also visited Great Britain in 1964, as a 4th Dan, for the B.K.F. There are only a few Karate-ka still actively training today in Britain who remember his fast, powerful and dignified style.

On his arrival in France, Master Harada was teaching a traditional, very straightforward Karate. Practice consisted mainly of 'Ten no Kata', kihon, Sanbon (three-step) kumite and kata. Whilst researches with Egami had certainly become part of his practice, these new-found benefits were being expressed through the university style he had been taught. The experiences with

Master Hiroo Mochizuki, the son of the famous Master Minoru Mochizuki. He visited Gt. Britain in 1964, and only a few British Karate-ka still actively training remember his fast, powerful, dignified style .

practitioners of Capoeira and boxing, for example, had made him further aware of the rigidity of the Shotokan he was practising. Although this form of training was deemed unnatural, Master Harada had not yet transformed the structure of practice.

Master Harada was unusual at this time in that, instead of merely counting, giving instructions, he would actually take part in the lesson. He would 'accept' (a word he uses often) each student in turn, blocking each attack. In this way, he not only built up a more intensive training atmosphere, but also a stronger, deeper bond with his students.

Master Ohshima had arranged for Master Harada's arrival, and had told him to contact Master Murakami. However, it was Hoang Nam who contacted Harada first, and organised a special course, to which came Master Harada's first students in Europe. Among those who attended were Marc Bassis, Daniel Shemla, Jean-Pierre Gerbolet and Francis Salomon, who had begun training under Ohshima. Henri Plee was also there, and Master Harada remembers him as being very friendly, astute and asking many questions. In a later interview, Plee noted that Harada, as a personal pupil to Egami, was extremely interesting, and remembered the Karate as being highly energetic with much stamina work, though limited in the number of techniques. With considerable foresight, Plee recalled that Harada's practice was always performed in an intelligent manner. During this period Master Harada was staying at a small hotel in the Avenue Port Royal, arranged for him by Hoang Nam. Master Harada was told that Master Murakami was out of the country and could not be contacted, but this was not true. One day, purely by accident, Harada visited a cheap Vietnamese restaurant behind the Panteon, and came face-to-face with Murakami! In those days, foreign communities in Paris were very small, and they all tended to congregate in the same location.

Every Monday evening, Master Harada would teach at Murakami's dojo in the rue Mercoeur, and Henri Plee's dojo in the rue de la Montagne-Sainte Genevieve, Paris. Just the previous year (1962) Plee's book, 'Karate by Pictures', had been published in English. The front cover showed a Japanese Karate-ka performing a powerful roundhouse kick.

Master Harada had been in France only a few short months before he was inexplicably deported to Belgium by the authorities. Professor Bernard Mathieu, a 5th Dan and academic from

The late Master Hoang Nam, a Vietnamese Karate teacher who ran a dojo in Paris, became the first Oriental to demonstrate the art in Gt. Britain. This was, in July 1958, under the auspices of Mr. Vernon Bell, who introduced Karate to the U.K. The above photo was taken in June 1972, during a training course Master Nam conducted in Tydlesley, Manchester.

the University of Rheims, and a student of Master Harada from 1964, has made a detailed study of what actually happened to cause this unfortunate and unsavoury incident. The author would like to quote directly from correspondence with Professor Mathieu as, in his own words, *"I'd feel happier if once and for all the truth could be officially published, even though I know that people always feel attracted to a bit of legend and mystery concerning people like Sensei. I think that it is an important episode since it changed the course of Sensei's life as it brought him to stay in Europe when he had planned to go back to Brazil... and had already built-up quite a following.*

"It all began, in fact, when Ohshima Sensei came over to France, invited by people within the French Judo Federation...to teach Karate, which had first been brought to their attention by an article published in 'Life' in 1956. Ohshima was, at the time, in California and accepted to come for a year only, but promised that before he went he would recommend someone. (In actual fact, Master Ohshima, who acted as Director of Technique, returned after some ten months due to Karate 'political problems' in the USA. Prior to that stay, he had visited in 1961/62, but had only taught for two weeks). *It turned out to be Harada Sensei who eventually accepted the invitation, though for a limited length of time too. At that time Karate was already spreading a little and in any case some people had already grasped that it could become something important, with an existence of its own and not within the Judo Federation. Thus ambitions were growing, some political, some economic, and soon tensions appeared... Unfortunately such a state of things does have a bearing on what was to happen later on as Harada Sensei literally landed in a world where not all people were interested only in discovering a new martial art. In many ways practice was not the main concern. Next to this, various 'Orientals' were already jumping on the bandwagon, as it were...*

"To understand fully the situation, one must remember that at the time, people from Asian countries, certainly Japan, were far from being in a financially advantageous position in Europe, as they had strict monetary control, and what they could get teaching Karate appeared as very comfortable indeed, but they had no officially-recognised position as yet.

"Anyhow, as soon as he arrived in Paris, Harada Sensei was met...(by Nam and later by Murakami)*...and they asked him not to join the French Federation, but to stay with them to form an association of their own, so that Karate should remain something really Japanese! Of course, all of Ohshima Sensei's pupils had started practising with Harada Sensei as soon as possible, and expected that, in the course of time, they would join a big demonstration — not quite a competition yet, though Ohshima had laid down the rules for them — a demonstration that the French authorities of the time were organising.*

"Harada Sensei was then torn between what he considered to be his duty to these young pupils and the pressure the two Oriental

The 'Funakoshi of Europe' — Master Henri Plee of France (left).

instructors were putting on him. Eventually he gave in to them, as he thought that these people who wanted to stay in France longer than he would, should be helped, and he managed to convince his pupils not to join the Federation group, promising he would help them to the best of his abilities. However, those were the days just after the Algerian war and control over immigrants was still pretty strong, and since three foreigners had decided to start up an association, there was a police inquiry. Each of them was called for an interview, to explain the reasons for their actions. Harada was asked various questions, including where he lived at the time and what were his motives for coming to France...

"Now, you must understand that it took us 20 years to get to the truth of what happened afterwards, since Harada Sensei was never told anything and he was given no explanation later, when he was expelled. The way we got to the bottom of things is through a pupil of ours who became a police inspector and worked for the Ministry

of the Interior. France has a highly-centralised administration and all these things are duly preserved, even long after it is over. Thus the police report mentions all the details about these interviews, including the letters written at the time, and I can tell you that it came as quite a shock to us to get this information, which unfortunately was not made public. All our previous queries over the years had remained fruitless. It turned out that, in their own interview...other...instructors had denied everything Harada Sensei had said, and in fact, declared that he was a dangerous character not to be trusted, and that he certainly wasn't staying with them when he arrived in France. The conclusion to the police report is simple: 'It does not seem advisable to renew Mr. Harada's permit.' So without any further ado, Harada Sensei was taken by the French police (handcuffed) to Gare du Nord and expelled to Belgium."

Strange as it might seem perhaps, a little more than one year later Ohshima's senior students, who had formed a club which they named '*Tekki Dojo*', and who had remained faithful to Harada, investigated the possibility of his being allowed back into France to teach on courses. The French police raised no objection, as no real motive was ever written in Harada's '*dossier de simple police*' (ordinary police file). What is particularly ironic was that, seven years later, Master Harada was instructing a special unit of the Monaco Police in Monte Carlo. There is a humorous aside here. The invitation was accepted and Harada made his way south from Paris to the Mediterranean coast. At his hotel in Monaco he had to fill-in the usual details and before long he was picked up by two plain-clothes detectives and taken to the police station.

Meanwhile, the Monaco police had called at his hotel to pick him up, and on hearing what had happened, sent their cars to find him. Of course all the time this was happening, he was in the police station. He was released and told to make his own way back. Princess Grace of Monaco was informed of the incident, and apologised personally to him — you see, he was there to train her bodyguards! Some years later Master Harada was to meet Prince Rainier. The Prince presented him with a medal for teaching the special security squad responsible for assuring the safety of VIPs in the Principality. This small token of thanks was, regrettably, stolen in England.

From the initial deportation episode, a number of stories sprang up, political in nature, surrounding Master Harada's

Master Harada demonstrates body evasion during a class in Brussels in the mid '60s. His assistant is Ken Waight, the master's first British uchi-deshi ('inside' student).

possible teaching of members of the OAS — Organisation Armee Secrete — a terrorist group who, opposed to the independence of Algeria, had supposedly planted bombs in Paris and elsewhere at the time of the Algerian war. The truth is, of course, far less dramatic, less romantic. A not-so-simple case of economic expediency perpetrated by certain individuals for their own gain. As Professor Mathieu continued: *"As you can see, the story is rather sad, and it is true that over the years Sensei has attracted an uncommon amount of jealousy...People in France and elsewhere have cheated him, taking advantage of his sincerity...when, in fact, I don't know many people who are as generous as he."*

The author, from his own experiences, can certainly add that Master Harada is a most generous person, he really does love to share, but Professor Mathieu sums-up this aspect very nicely once again. Following a very major split in 1972 in the group to which Master Harada was associated, all that was left was a club in Macon and two individuals. *"Jean Marie Dupont and I were students at the time and, of course, chronically short of money. So Sensei would take advantage of his trips to other countries to stop over in Paris, at his own expense, to practice with us in an old garage. Of course, there's no counting the number of times he took us to restaurants then and now."* There are many such incidences. The author will provide one more: Following the re-establishment of relations with the French Federation, Master Harada was asked to give a series of courses in three different cities. He was duly paid, and proceeded to give one-third of the money back to help the Karate-Do Shotokai France association.

Master Harada was expelled to Belgium at the end of June 1963. He caught the train for Brussels, then moved into Holland and north to a city built largely upon piles driven into the marshes, 96 islands joined by 300 bridges — Amsterdam. Continually followed by the police, he travelled south-east and entered West Germany, visiting Dusseldorf on the River Rhine, before heading north-east to the large seaport of Hamburg. A great industrial and commercial centre on the River Elbe, 85 miles upstream from the North Sea, Hamburg had recently suffered severe flooding caused by gales. Harada then returned to Brussels in August. It was the summer holidays in Europe and the dojos were closed. Master Harada had decided to make the most of his stay and toured the four countries, lodging in small family-run hotels and visiting museums, art galleries and so on. He expected, after all, to be returning to Brazil. He had money from selling his flat and cashing-in his pension fund from the bank.

Since his Waseda days he had wanted to see, first-hand, the work of the great French impressionist painters. In Paris, his pupils had been pleased to take him to the galleries, and he stood

Master Harada pictured with Julien Naessens (left), the Aikido sensei, Masamichi Noro, and Mrs. Naessens in Brussels, 1963.

in wonderment at paintings by Monet, Pissarro, Renoir and particularly the highly original post-impressionist Paul Cezanne. But the artists that really captured his attention were the fauvist painter Henri Matisse, regarded by many as the most important painter of the 20th Century, and the cubists, Pablo Picasso and Georges Braque. He spent his time valuably. But the hounding by the authorities was an uncalled-for nuisance and it blighted his holiday — of this there is little doubt.

As fate would have it, he met a student whom he had taught whilst in France, walking along a street in Brussels. This fortuitously led to a meeting with Master Masamichi Noro, an Aikido 6th Dan (which had been awarded in January that year), who had started his training at the Aikikai under O'Sensei Morihei Ueshiba. Before moving to Europe in August 1961 as an official Aikikai instructor with his senior, 45-year-old Master Masahiro Nakazono (also a 6th Dan Aikido and 5th Dan Judo, and Chief Instructor (Aikido) of the International Budo Council), Master Noro had been an assistant instructor at the Aikikai in Tokyo, and teacher of the Aikido section of the Japanese Navy. Cognisant of the position that Master Harada had found himself in, Master Noro introduced him to Julien Naessens, who managed to obtain a three-month breathing space from the authorities. During this period, Master Harada lived with Naessens and his wife in their house on the outskirts of Brussels.

43-year-old Naessens, 5th Dan, was a leading figure in Belgian Judo, also a 3rd Dan in Aikido and 1st Dan Karate. Naessens (who is now dead) could be considered the Belgian equivalent of Henri Plee, namely the individual responsible for introducing Karate to that country. Among a number of positions held, he was at the time President of both the Federation Belge de Karatedo and the Ligue Belge d'Aikido, and Director of the Federation Belge de Judo. He was Vice-President of the Association Culturelle Europeenne d'Aikido, and Technical Secretary of the International Budo Council. Additionally he founded the review 'Judo Efficience'. Naessens was an influential man, but in November of 1963 Harada's three months were up. Naessens and Master Harada, accompanied by their lawyer, met officials at the Japanese Embassy in Brussels, with a view to seeing if Master Harada's stay could be extended. The Embassy was unable to intervene and, with expulsion imminent, Naessens contacted his teacher, Master Kenshiro Abbe, in Britain.

Why, one asks, did Master Harada not go back to Brazil, where life had gone well for him? Well, of course, as has already been mentioned, he did not wish to go back to the bank, but there was a deeper reason, and this was connected with the values associated with being Japanese. He had been expelled from France for no good reason, and felt that he had lost face and was determined to clear his name — it was a matter of honour. In truth he had to put up with considerable hardship later, when he moved to London. This episode is quite telling of Master Harada's quiet determination. He never once wrote to his family requesting assistance. It was normal practice at the bank, when an employee left, to have a collection and make them a gift of money. However, the unstable nature and poor exchange rate of the Brazilian cruzeiro caused problems, so he was given a few precious stones, sapphires, instead. One of these he gave to his sister, the other to the wife of David Delderfield for her birthday. Delderfield, who studied Judo and Kendo, was the caretaker of a school/youth centre in Acton, and he allowed Harada to use the school flat (the school hall acted as a personal dojo) without paying, as he had no money.

After Harada was expelled from France, Master Ogasahara of the Shito-Ryu visited, but stayed only six months. Master Yoshinao Nanbu of the Shukokai followed, then Master Taiji Kase of the Shotokan finally settled in Paris in 1967, where he

Taiji Kase, one of the three surviving Karate masters
that Harada greatly respects.

Master Kase (left) and Master Hiroshi Shirai left the JKA (Japan Karate Association) to form their own Shotokan organisation.

still lives with his wife and two daughters.

Taiji Kase is one of three living masters of Karate that Harada greatly respects (the others being Hirokazu Kanazawa, 9th Dan Shotokan and the Okinawan, Morio Higaonna, 8th Dan Goju-Ryu, upon both of whom much has been written). Born on the 9th February 1929 in Tokyo, Taiji Kase first trained at the Shotokan in 1944 as a marine cadet, and was at that time a 2nd Dan in Judo, having studied from the age of six. An interview in the French martial arts magazine '*Budo Europe*' many years ago provides a graphic account of the intensive training which Kase attended at the end of the war, when the fear of invasion was upon the country. Two years Harada's senior, he was graded to 3rd Dan in 1949, at the very young age of 20, and was Captain of Senshu University's Karate club for three years. The senior JKA representative in Europe until recently, Master Kase, along with Master Hiroshi Shirai (based in Italy), left the JKA to form their own Shotokan organisation. Master Kase is a teacher with traditional values, always approaching training with great enthusiasm. It is interesting to note that, like Harada, Master Kase reportedly has a love of old Budo books and philosophy, and both share the same favourite kata — '*Enpi*' and '*Meikyo*'.

After a gap of ten years, Master Harada and Master Kase met in late 1993 in Lisbon, and talked of old times over a meal. "*It was very nice,*" Harada said, "*very nice*".

5

Great Britain Becomes Home

The great Judo Master Kenshiro Abbe, 8th Dan (1915-1986). Abbe founded the British Judo Council in 1955 and the International Budo Council in 1958, and then, in 1963, invited Master Harada to England to teach Karate. He was also a 6th Dan in Aikido, having studied under Morihei Ueshiba, and held Dan ranks in four other martial arts.

Master Kenshiro Abbe, 8th Dan, came to England in 1955 to become Chief Instructor to the London Judo Society. He founded the British Judo Council that same year and then the International Budo Council in 1958. It was at his invitation that Master Harada came to England to teach Karate in 1963. Abbe, who was born in 1915, was an exceptional Judoka. He started training in 1929, gained his 1st Dan in 1930, and was graded to 5th Dan in 1934, the youngest-ever to do so, whilst attending the Special Budo College in Kyoto, from which he graduated in first place. With a host of important championship titles to his name, he became Judo instructor to the police in Osaka, the High School in Kyoto, and the Special Judo College of the Dai Nippon Butokukai. By 1938 he had reached 6th Dan (again the youngest-ever to have done so), and by 1945 7th Dan. In 1949 he became Chief Instructor to the Kyoto Police and Doshisha University. He became Editor of the *'Japanese Judo Magazine'* and Director of the Judo Social League. Abbe was a Budoka of superior credentials — let there be no mistake. He was also a 6th Dan in Aikido, having studied under Morihei Ueshiba, and held Dan ranks in Karate-Do, Kyudo (archery) and Ju-Kenjutsu (bayonet fighting) and received a 3rd Dan in Kendo at his first grading!

Standing 5ft, 8ins. in height and weighing some 11 stone, Abbe insisted that he had no particular natural aptitude for the martial arts. Rather, his achievements were the result of much hard work, and no small amount of blood, sweat and tears. He developed his own philosophy of *Kyu-Shin-Do* which, in essence, was the search for the truth which lies within us all. The three principal precepts to this philosophy were: all of nature is in a constant state of motion (*banbutsu ruten*); that such motion is rhythmical and flowing *(ritsu-do)*; and that all things work in harmony (*chowa*).

The National Judo Championships were held at the Royal Albert Hall, London, on Saturday the 23rd November 1963, in aid of the *'Freedom From Hunger Campaign'*. Along with Judo, the programme revealed that spectators would see a number of demonstrations, including Kendo (Tomio Otani and the British Kendo Council), Aikido (Masahiro Nakazono, 6th Dan; Masamichi Noro, 6th Dan; and the British Aikido Council) and Karate. There were many guests of honour, including the Earl of Lanesborough; Mr. Fugisaki, Minister of the Japanese Embassy;

Mr. Duncan, General Secretary of the British Olympic Association; and Mr. Jazarin, President of the French Black Belt Association. In the introduction to the 'Souvenir Programme', the President of the British Judo Council, Master Abbe, wrote that: *"As well as the finals of the Championship you will have the opportunity of seeing the finest exponents of the Japanese Martial Arts in Europe. I welcome and thank the many people who have travelled from many parts in order that we may see their skill. They are experts and Teachers of the International Budo Council."* There were 22 events that evening and the demonstration of '*Karate (combat without weapons)*' given by Master Harada, was number 16 — following the Judo heavyweight final, which was won by J. Gallon, and before '*Kendo no kata (formal sword play — real swords used)*', demonstrated by Tomio Otani and David Delderfield. Amongst other demonstrators that night were Kenshiro Abbe, Maku Michigami (7th Dan), Masutaro Otani (7th Dan) and Julien Naessens. Another Belgian 5th Dan, Jean Stas, was unable to participate due to injury.

A picture of some of these masters, of which Master Harada was one, appeared on the cover of Volume 1, Number 2 (January-February 1964) of '*Judo News*', and a report of the Championships and demonstrations was given by W. S. Wood, then General Secretary of the British Judo Council, who wrote: *"Mr. Harada, 5th Dan Karate, then treated us to a demonstration of Karate. Mr. Harada moves so fast that I found it impossible to count the number of times that he struck his opponent after being attacked. Mr. Vanderdonckt, who substituted for Mr. Naessens at very short notice, deserved the sympathy of all when he attacked Mr. Harada."* John Gargin, General Secretary of the Federation of British Judo Organisations, writing in the same magazine remarked that: *"The largest Association in the Federation, the British Judo Council has...just put on at the Royal Albert Hall in London, a Japanese Martial Arts Display which, in my opinion, was second to none in its presentation and appeal"*. Certainly it was a near-capacity audience, and the display was regarded as probably the finest in the history of British martial arts.

Master Harada remembers the demonstration well, but was rather disappointed as it did not go as he had planned. He per-formed his favourite kata, '*Enpi*', but the kumite demonstration was badly flawed because his assistant didn't turn up until the last moment. A new assistant had to be found, and nothing seemed to go as planned in front of the audience of 8,000, due quite simply to insufficient practice with the assistant. Master Harada recalled that, when he performed *gedan-barai*, his opponent, who was very experienced in Judo and Aikido, fell over — which, of course, he wasn't supposed to do!

The above edition of '*Judo News*' is particularly noteworthy, for it contains the only article on Karate written to date by Master Harada. This short piece, entitled '*The Essence of Karate*', is of considerable value historically and it gives an insight into the master's thinking at the time. In the article, he explained that Europeans were restricted in their Karate as they lacked experience, and that progress would be on a trial-and-error basis and thus slow. He noted that a compounded problem had arisen in that certain Japanese instructors had not been teaching within a scientific framework. Master Harada considered the dynamics of training in terms of three factors: speed, strength and endurance. Different arts and sports, he suggested, placed greater emphasis on these three factors. In Karate, Harada explained, the factors arranged in their order of importance were: speed, endurance and strength. Because Karate does not require a great deal of strength (as, for example, does the 100 yards race), it suits the Japanese, he said. The master continued by noting the four important elements of Karate training: correct form of posture, relaxation, concentration and natural movement, and concluded on an encouraging note where he stated that he felt European Karate could become as proficient as Japan, once the fundamental principles were understood.

Master Harada took a course in Karate at the Abbe School of Judo, in the basement dojo in Judd Street, near King's Cross, on the weekend of the 7th and 8th of December 1963, and subsequently was asked to give a large number of courses and demonstrations around the country. From early 1964 until 1968, Harada was, in fact, alternating between Britain and Brussels every three months. The organiser for these Belgian courses was Julien Naessens. Naessens was business-orientated and wanted, Harada explained, to expand into France, Holland and later West Germany. Master Harada never liked him, and their relationship was purely a working one. Naessens arranged the courses and provided the students, whilst Harada taught. They would split the profits 50/50.

Master Harada cited two stories that stick in his mind about

Naessens. The first involved Harada grading a number of students to black-belt, and then presenting them with the coveted belt. *"Naessens didn't like this. He was very upset,"* Harada said. *"He wanted them to buy the belts at his martial arts shop."* The second involved going out for a meal to a restaurant after one evening's training. Naessens was angry that they didn't go to his bar — and everyone pay for his alcohol! Master Harada noted that not too long afterwards, Naessens reneged on a verbal contract, and he never taught at his dojo again, nor had anything else to do with him.

Ken Waight, Master Harada's first black-belt and *uchi-deshi* ('inside' student) in this country, accompanied and assisted the master on many courses over a six-year period from 1964 to 1979. On one trip to Brussels he remembers: *"I knew that there was some friction between Julien Naessens and Harada. I felt that he wanted Sensei to teach in a certain way, one which suited Naessens' set-up. Maybe this is too simple an explanation, but I think Naessens' dojo was not dedicated solely to authentic training. There seemed to be a lot of 'politicking' going on in the background as well."* Waight continued: *"I arrived at the dojo with one other Shodan from Britain. We walked into the lounge area, a bar/cafe, where Harada was sitting amongst a group of students. We sat down and ordered a coffee. I took in the surroundings — quite different from The Hut!* (see shortly). *I was not used to such elaborate comfort in a dojo after being brought-up in the austere atmosphere of the dojo in Britain. I saw Sensei getting slightly agitated and knew what was to follow. Harada was always ready to show that any time was the time to teach and practice. He asked me to deliver a series of tsukis* (punches). *Dressed in my best suit and trying to avoid the coffee tables, we demonstrated some 'points' he wanted to put across to the onlookers. So the stage was set for the weekend. Actually, the real point he wanted to put across to this dojo was his authentic training.*

"Marc (Bassis) *was also given the full works, no holds barred, in order to show this group how we practised with true spirit. I can still remember the face of a 1st degree black-belt from there, who made the mistake of pointing out something about kumite. I think his grade had been a present, and now he was shown what it was really worth. He looked as if he could hardly stand after finishing a series of ippon kumite with Sensei Harada."*

On one of these trips to Brussels, Master Harada met Jotaro

Grange Farm, 1966. One of Harada's top students in France, Marc Bassis, is on the far left and Ken Waight is on the other side of the Master.

Takegi, a graduate in economics from Chuo University, who is now Chief Instructor to the Shotokai in Japan. Master Takegi was on a business trip to Europe, and he showed Harada new developments from Tokyo in Naessens' dojo. *"These were very interesting,"* Harada recalled, and for six months toward the end of 1967 and the beginning of 1968, he returned to Tokyo to investigate. He trained with Master Takegi three or four times and learned many things. But overall it was not a good trip. Master Harada needed advice, was uncertain about the direction Shotokai was taking, and visited Master Egami to inquire as to his position — Shotokai or Shinwa Taido. But Master Egami never gave an answer, he sat on the fence, and this depressed Master Harada greatly, for he felt that his teacher had let him down yet again. Egami spoke of his student, Hiroyuki Aoki, and noted that Aoki was *"the best Karate-ka in the world"* (to use Harada's recollection of Egami's words), but Egami would not allow Harada to meet him. *"I felt very jealous of Aoki,"* Harada openly admitted. However, one thing that was sorted out was that, as Master Harada was no longer going to return to Brazil, a replacement had to be found. Master Egami chose Arinobu Ishibata, a graduate of Chuo, to take Harada's place.

The British Judo Council's national summer training school was held at the Grange Farm Centre in Chigwell, Essex. Four consecutive one-week courses were arranged from the 1st to the 29th of August 1964. Master Harada took the third week, with Masters Abbe and Yakoto (4th Dan). All courses were heavily subscribed to (each course was restricted to 150 students), and all Budoka were welcome, regardless of grade or affiliation. It might interest readers to know that a week's course, including meals and accommodation, could be had for the princely sum of £9.00. The Grange Farm Centre was subsequently the venue for the annual Shotokai Summer School until 1972, when the University of Keele was chosen. Since that time a number of university campuses have provided the venue. The Summer School at Grange Farm, 1970, was an important one for Karate-Do Shotokai, and followers of Master Harada's training, for it was on that course that Harada decided, after much soul-searching and dissatisfaction, to revert back to early 1950s training.

Master Egami was a figurehead for the Shotokai, the Chief Instructor, but he couldn't practice because of his ill-health. (Egami became a spiritual mentor to students after this, taking on an almost god-like quality in the eyes of some of his pupils). After his heart-attack, practice changed quite drastically when led by later students. These students were well-intentioned, of this there seems little doubt, and the theories they were adhering to potentially offered much — they were based on Egami's, after all. But as Egami wrote: *"Theory is not sufficient: you must learn with your body"* (*'The Heart of Karate-Do'*, Kodansha: 1980). Or, as Funakoshi noted: *"The true nature of Karate-Do cannot be explained in words even if one's efforts with pen or tongue are carried to the point of exhaustion and beyond"* (*'Karate-Do Nyumon'*, Kodansha: 1988).

But Egami's disabilities meant that students could not actually feel practice, and Harada said that is where things went wrong, for Egami's ideas were advanced, abstract, and difficult to concretize physically. As we know, these 'new' techniques (I place 'new' in inverted commas because Yoshitaka, Shimoda and Okuyama, for example, knew of them), were flexible, fluid, liquid, never stopping abruptly. Only when there is no feeling of power is the blow effective. Harada actually experienced it when he and Egami were researching this method of practice. Harada said that subsequent generations were denied this all-important practical reference. The problem was compounded by the nature of the techniques, for as Egami noted: *"The point is that*

Master Harada side-steps an attack made by Steve Hope and counters with a hook-punch.

the effectiveness of a blow cannot be discovered simply from its appearance. And herein lies one difficulty in practising" ('*The Heart of Karate-Do*', Kodansha: 1980).

At the time, Master Harada believed in the directions that were coming from the Shotokai under Egami's headship, and hearing of important changes invited French instructors, who had recently returned from Japan, to come to England for a course, so that all could learn and pick-up on the changes. In France "*They started getting us to do long sessions of bunny-hopping, warm-ups which lasted sometimes more than an hour and were, in fact, more in line with survival tests than Karate practice. Still, we accepted it all because, in some way, we thought we would be much better afterwards. But in terms of the practice proper, because the idea was to let your body's energy go forward and not to have stiff, fixed postures, all our weight would move to the front leg in a most excruciating manner*" (Professor Mathieu). The event was described as "*An experience, but not to be done again*". Master Harada said that the training was a real eye-opener. "*Bunny-hopping two or three miles. No! Bad training.*"

One of the 'survivors' of these early week-long Summer Schools was Stephen Hope, 5th Dan, now Master Harada's longest-serving senior grade in Great Britain. He describes the first Summer School he attended so: *"The facilities were extremely basic. There were ten people to a billet, sleeping on two-tier bunk beds. Resting and sleeping was difficult at best. The French contingent, who were at the time the largest group, brought their own food, as the food served in the canteen was considered by them to be inedible. The toilet and washing facilities were outside. Sensei shared the same facilities, though he usually had the seniors in his billet. The first practice started at 6.00 a.m. This came about apparently because Sensei wished to discourage excessive drinking in the evenings, so that people would keep their best condition for every practice. In some years there were over 150 people attending; even so Sensei would know if someone was absent at the morning practice. Seniors were dispatched to ensure the individual attended in double-quick time.*

"The main hall was unavailable at that time in the morning, so we would practice outside. The dew from the grass on bare feet was, on some mornings, so cold that your feet were numb. Not long after the start of the practice the sun would start to rise and you quickly became an expert in judging the sun's height in the sky when it would be 8.00 and the end of the first practice of the day..."

The French, being the largest and most experienced group, aided Master Harada in the organisation and teaching on the course. The next-largest group was from Scotland. Steve Hope remembers that *"There was always rivalry between the two groups, which had a tendency to erupt at any time. I was told that Sensei would patrol the campus in an open-top car with a bo at the ready, to discourage any trouble. I was also told of an incident when a water-fight broke out between the two groups, and several people found themselves on the wrong end of Sensei's bo."*

Ken Waight used to assist Master Harada on these early *gasshuku,* and spoke of the primitive accommodation in the wooden barrack-type huts, and the poor food. *"But the keiko (practice) made up for any lack in comfort, in fact, perhaps the rather spartan conditions helped us. These were the first real gasshuku to be held in Britain for Harada's group. By that I mean eating, sleeping and practising together. And what practice it was! All of the leaders and keen students attended, and Harada was to impress on us what special training was all about. He told stories of his hard training at Waseda and the gasshuku he attended, and it felt like we were there to re-live some of those moments. For the*

Master Harada, surrounded by students, during special night-time practice at Grange Farm in 1967.

general students there were three keiko each day, for Dan grades four. Spread over six days, this usually meant between about seven or eight hours daily practice, often finishing at ten in the evening. There was not much time for any socialising or a beer at the end of the day, as the nearest pub was some way down the road, outside the complex. So for the Dan grades or assistants, the day finished off with a shower, then bed, which most of us felt ready for anyway."

Ken Waight continued: *"For the people who went to Grange Farm in those early days, there must be many a tale to tell. I can still recall some of the faces now. One humorous encounter that will stay with me forever was the student who always asked 'Where does the power come from?' He usually asked this when Sensei was demonstrating his tsuki. Being the assistant, I was immediately asked to stand at the front of a line of students whilst he elaborated and showed penetrating power. This was often shown with mawashi-geri. Well, as you might expect, I became a little fed-up when this particular bright-spark came up with this question yet again. So one day, when he put this question forward once more, I quickly invited him up to see for himself. Harada Sensei was looking on, and I said convincingly that I wanted to feel his tsuki. I stood behind him with my arms held out ready, for I knew what was going to take place. As Harada let go with a soft, penetrating tsuki, the young man just collapsed into my arms. Legs buckling under him, he slumped back, then down. He went white as I held him. Slowly I brought him to his feet and led him to the back of the class.*

"I recall the time when, at almost every keiko we would practice endless tsuki through low kiba-dachi. For 20, 30, 40 minutes punches would flow from our hips as we struggled to keep extended in low posture. Students would fall, crawl, get up and start again. I remember doing this for over one hour sometimes. From this low posture we would move immediately into zenkutsu and continue tsuki, this time with less form and more movement. Extension came naturally, unconsciously, as we emptied our bodies into the never-stopping movement. What came out of this was a new connection with our waza (technique), *deep and graceful movement with long, open extension. Another practice in which we were involved at about the time was almost the opposite. Here we developed deep concentration in a calm, unmoving way. With our arms extended, we would breathe slowly in, as we extended and raised our hands, fingers open, then, equally, we would breathe out as the wrists were flexed downward. This would continue very slowly for up to 30 minutes without interruption. A patient way of working to build concentration, and energy was needed for this type of practice. Gradually, out of this, came a very strong feeling of energy and extension through our arms and legs."*

Steve Hope noted that: *"Many people began to appreciate the value gained from long, intensive periods practicing with Sensei, such as at Summer School, which prompted some clubs in the early 1980s to hold month-long club courses with Sensei. usually there were practices most evenings during the week, with weekend courses in-between. The month ended, invariably, with a National black-belt course or an executive course* (2nd Dan and above)... *It was a period of great development for all concerned. It allowed Sensei time with individuals and to explore and explain many things to a greater depth than ever before. There was an explosion of innovative ideas, the results of which are only beginning to materialise now."*

Prior to this, in May 1979, Master Harada and some of the seniors attended a special weekend course in transactional analysis. This course had a profound effect upon Master Harada and altered his approach to teaching. It was also at this time that the notion of movement, as viewed as an ability, came into prominence within the KDS, to be practised and acquired like any other technique. Explorations on this theme became a major cornerstone of modern Shotokai practice, and Master Harada's training entered a new dimension, *"evolving years later in Sensei's ability to stop or break an attacker without touching"* (S. Hope).

Harada's Karate group was part of the International Budo Council for only a few years. In 1966, Master Abbe returned to Japan, having for a long time missed his family, and things were not quite the same again. Master Harada did not see eye-to-eye with Masutaro O'Tani, a 7th Dan Judoka, over the development of Karate within the IBC. Master O'Tani had an exceptional lineage, having started Judo in 1917 under Master Seizo Usui. He studied under many famous masters, including Aida, Tani, Hata, Kabumoto, Ishiguro and Kotani. He was graded by Master Shuichi Nagaoka, 10th Dan. He first came to England in 1919, and had been Judo instructor to the universities of Oxford and Cambridge for 11 years before becoming instructor at the Anglo-Japanese Club in 1932.

Master Harada remembered Master Abbe with great affection. He was a powerful Judoka, *"quiet, shy and very, very good,"* Harada said. Abbe was also something of an eccentric by all accounts. Harada recalled that at his home, Abbe kept birds but disliked cages, and allowed them to fly freely around the house. Harada cannot forget the copious amount of bird droppings, here, there and everywhere! On another occasion, Master Abbe bought two goats in Shepherd's Bush Market, and would take them for a walk, each on a lead. Abbe died on the 1st of December 1986, aged 71. He is remembered fondly throughout British Judo.

Feeling unhappy with the situation in which he found himself, Master Harada resigned from the IBC and formed the Karate-Do Shotokai (KDS) Association. The initial association had some ten clubs up and down Great Britain, and a membership of perhaps 200 to 250. These clubs had regular courses and Master Harada, who has never had his own dojo in this country, would travel to them. He would also train at Kenneth Williams' dojo in Hillingdon, first once, then twice, and finally three times a week until about 1970. 'The Hut', located in the West Drayton road, as this dojo was known, having previously been used by scouts, was basic in the extreme. During the depths of winter, training was difficult as there was no heating, and they had to put coins in a meter to get electricity for lighting. In the summer, the heat in the converted wooden building was stifling. There were some five or six students training with Harada initially, though later numbers grew to about 25 as Karate became better-known.

Ken Waight remembers The Hut and Master Harada's training well: "*If The Hut itself was not-so-grand, the spirit there was. Abbe Sensei had taught there, and later, Senseis Noro, Nakazono and Chiba. There was always an enthusiastic spirit and warm camaraderie. The keiko was strong…It was here that I really started my apprenticeship in Karate with him (1964) and also where the first group of Shodan came from. I remember his early classes and the emphasis on scientific explanations to support his ideas… However, the main thrust of his teaching was to create precision with speed, softness and penetration. This was demonstrated time and time again. The other main area to which we were exposed was the practice of slow, deep, continuous kihon(basic training). This developed a very strong central power. It was one of the practises that was to influence and stay with me for many years. We were told to breathe very slowly, with long outbreaths, and to extend through the movement. Really it was like walking meditation. This kihon lasted 30 to 40 minutes without a break, in very low zenkutsu…We practiced countless hours, developing precision in form, feeling extension of breath and of movement. I began to understand that this practice was a way of transforming energy.*"

Accompanying his teacher about once a fortnight, assisting on courses in Scotland, Wales, the West Country, Kent and the Midlands, where these early dojos were beginning to appear, Ken Waight received literally hundreds of hours of private practice with Master Harada. "*We used to call him the Wild Boar,*" Waight recalls, "*because of his Chinese birth sign, and also he was so very strong. Training as a close assistant to Harada was demanding. I believe that he really wanted to impress on us Europeans what true Karate practise was, and he set about it in a determined way. As his assistant I was his partner in almost all of the demonstrations at that time. I cannot forget the countless times that he impressed on students what he felt was needed in order for them to grasp a certain point. He loved to show again and again through his waza what was essential. It felt to me as if half the time spent at the courses was given over to demonstrations. At least, that's what my body told me. Harada Sensei would never hold back in his demonstrations, whether he was showing yoko kekomi* (side-thrust kick), *shuto* (knife-hand), *uchi* (striking), *tsuki* (punching), *etc. I still remember the thrust of his foot to my midriff or the uchi komi to my biceps. I think that through all of these situations he was also working out his*

Master Harada leads a class in Hampshire.

own ideas, much as an artist would make sketches before developing a finished painting.

"Training this way was unique. Looking back on it, I was fortunate to be in the right place at the right time to participate, although at the time I sometimes wondered what I was letting myself in for. It was a very creative time for him, as I can still recall many times he tried new kimachi (feeling) in his tsuki, or researched other ways to receive attacks with soft movements. I usually stood at the front of the group of students who were there to feel his penetration tsuki. There could be three, four or eight people lined up to catch his 'feeling'. This was demonstrated time and time again, much to my intestines' delight. Gradually, through this type of inner apprenticeship, I absorbed the practice as well as developing a soft but deep resilience in my body. I could receive again and again the waza of this sensei into my body and return back, ready either to follow his gorei (expert group training) or, once again, demonstrate with him.

"On the return journeys by train back to London I don't think I could have been much company for him. I was usually in quite a silent state, feeling what was the left-over of the deep penetrating waza that had been on the menu that weekend in my body. Usually I felt quite empty, not in a negative way, just emptied out and very

relaxed. Now it might seem to people who have never entered this type of training with a teacher, that this was a needlessly brutal way to practice. But in fact, this was the Eastern way to transmit from body to body the essence of the keiko, as long as it embodied a life philosophy and was not just built around technique and power, which could be distorted or misunderstood. His Karate, as he often said, was one of human relationship.

"*I think that in order to develop that quality, the dissolving of our ego, along with the use of external strength, is necessary. This is what he was to give to me — a deep way to live through my body experience of the keiko. It was something that went beyond words or ideas, and an experience about which there were no questions to ask. That life philosophy was there in the daily practice I had with him, the exchange, the kindness, the dedication, the perseverance and concern in developing clear, sincere practice.*

"*However, Harada Sensei was only really severe and demanding with his close students, and ones he felt could understand, or were ready for that type of teaching. Mostly he was patient, warm and convivial, although he could be aroused easily if a misunderstanding was taking place.*" Waight remembers that Harada, during the Sixties, "*had a lively but remote air about him, perhaps because he knew few people here, and coming only recently to Europe, was unfamiliar with the customs and feelings that we have. However, as I was to find out, Harada Sensei, although a man always ready to laugh, to tell a tale, and who exuded a warm atmosphere, nonetheless always kept an inner distance.*"

When Ken Waight left the KDS in 1970, he took his first trip to Japan in the Spring of that year. Master Harada had written to Master Egami as a form of introduction for his student. Waight was fortunate enough to meet and have a meal at Master Egami's house on a number of occasions, and trained under him at the dojo of both Gakushuin and Chuo universities. As the finest British student of Master Harada at the time, it is worth recounting Waight's first experience at Gakushuin and a 'minor' problem he encountered afterwards as a direct result.

"*It was Saturday and very humid. I had heard of the extremely demanding practice...but I wasn't prepared for what followed. After 30 minutes of very strenuous warm-ups, which included lots of painful low jumping, running, etc., we sat down in seiza. As I didn't know any Japanese then, I tried to follow what was going on by quick visual reference. We sat in one line and the captain strode out*

Hiroyuki Aoki: "The best Karate-ka in the world" according to
Master Shigeru Egami, as recollected by Harada.

to the centre of the dojo and demonstrated mae-geri, which started
from a squat position, legs open, and ended with a fully extended
jodan geri. He walked back. I waited. Nothing happened. Then, suddenly, there was a shout, at which everyone went into motion. Let me
just say that the rest of the keiko, which lasted a further one-and-a-
half hours, consisted of thousands of these squat kicks. I still remember people crawling, shouting, jumping for what seemed an endless
time. What a terrific spirit they had, and what energy!

"The next day when I woke up, I went to move, but found nothing responded. It was as if I was paralysed. Just my neck turned. I
rolled it, then started to feel the rest of my painful body. Gradually I
turned over out of the futon. It took me some minutes to stand. My
first priority was to go to the toilet. Now Japanese toilets are not
designed to be used by stiff and painful foreigners, being both small
and arranged so you have to squat down. Half of the toilet bowl
extended over a raised diagonal portion, which meant one had to

balance oneself carefully and delicately over the bowl — not the ideal position when one had legs like mine which could hardly move. After falling off, later I devised a way by tying my obi (belt) to the waterpipe and lowering myself down with it! It now makes me smile, but it didn't feel too funny then."

Although training in Japan was very hard and he enjoyed the spirit of practice, Waight felt that something was missing. *"I think that being used to a teacher much older and more experienced had allowed me to gain subtle insights into keiko. That was what I felt was missing at the University practice. Occasionally a sempai (senior) would make a visit, but generally the sessions were run by the captain and fourth-year students. This meant that there was a particular way we always practised. The experience of older teachers was missing."* Waight realised, at this stage, that he was not finding that which he had gone to Japan to seek. But later, at Chuo, he met Aoki, and that, *"Opened up the horizons through which I could experience and develop my practice and help liberate my own practice from the restrictions that had come to be taken for granted".* This led to Waight returning to Japan for five more years. Later he became interested in Zen, Oriental medicine, Acupuncture and Shiatsu, and consolidated all he had learned into a system of movement. He founded the British School of Oriental Therapy and Movement, which is currently based in West Dulwich, London.

But what of Egami's comment to Harada about *"the best Karate-ka in the world"*? Master Harada has never seen Aoki, but Waight lived and trained with Aoki's group, called Rakutenkai, for two years, and got to know Master Aoki particularly well. One of Waight's fellow-students (there were some 15 to 20 at any one time) was Egami's son, Masatake. Waight recalled: *"Aoki had great charisma, was very artistically inclined, radical, flamboyant and eclectic. Far from being a classicist, he researched into the old, new, art culture, whatever way his inspiration took him in order to find new ways of movement through the martial arts…He had developed an integrated system of martial arts called Sogo Budo (a synthesis of movement through martial arts). Aoki was greatly gifted technically as can be seen in the book on kata that he was the model for. There are over 50 kata in here, along with bo. Anybody who fails to be impressed must surely be blind. But more than his exceptional technical gifts, he had artistic vision which enabled him to see deeply into the world of martial arts movement and create*

Master Shigeru Egami (1912-1982).

something new out of it. Perhaps it was this same gift as well as his character that led many of his students into confusion, as there were many difficulties in working with this teacher. Later, many of his older, talented leaders left."

When Egami died in 1982 (Harada had a telephone call from a friend from Gakushuin University), Harada said that he had experienced very mixed feelings. He knew Egami was very ill and remembered all the good times and the special practice, but he had not given him direction when requested, and Harada felt cheated. From that point onward, without certain direction from

Master Harada demonstrates how force is channelled using black-belt students.

*The laws of physics will ensure that the unsuspecting last in the line
will shortly feel the force of Harada's punch!*

Master Egami, he reverted back to the orthodox method of his university days, which included, of course, the invaluable year-and-a-half with Egami. The 1971 Summer Course, already mentioned, provided the turning point to a more orthodox style. Whilst this was welcomed by many, others decided to follow in the way they had been practising and this led to an inevitable major split. But Master Harada was now his own man. Three or four years had been spent in unsuccessful experimentation — he knew when to draw the line. Harada studied his own background and Karate-Do in great depth, and changes slowly began to appear.

Counting aloud stopped. This is an aspect of training which is so obvious that few people think of it. Harada explained that Master Funakoshi, being a teacher of children, had taught in a 'teacher-type' fashion, and no-one thought about it. It was just accepted. But this method of instruction conditions the student to sound, neglecting, or at least relegating, the visual. Harada then stood in front of the class attacking or retreating suddenly, and the class would have to match his step. This type of practice is physically and emotionally exhausting as one is required to concentrate continuously, but it teaches perceptivity and much more. In fact, with Master Harada, the student has a unique opportunity, for he may get a genuine glimpse of 1950s training, with the addition of 50 years of practice and personal evolution.

Returning to Britain early in 1968, after his unfulfilling trip to Tokyo, Master Harada rented a one-room flat in Muswell Hill, North London, and stayed until 1970. He was being called upon to travel widely in Europe now, at least once a month, and decided to move to Ealing so that he could be nearer Heathrow Airport, thus avoiding the traffic on a regular basis. He took a spacious top-floor flat just off Ealing Common and remained there until 1987. Forced to leave his home of 17 years when his flat was severely damaged by burst pipes, he then moved to another flat in Ealing Broadway for a year. There were complications surrounding his top floor flat however, and legal advice was taken. Ziggy Boban, 5th Dan, helped his teacher through this difficult time. Boban remembers, *"Sensei said that he had not realised how vulnerable he was, and that he would not have been able to organise these things himself. I also considered that we had been too protective of Sensei here in the UK, and he was too dependent on us. I believe that following these events and subsequent changes to the*

"... With Master Harada, the student has a unique opportunity, for he may get a genuine glimpse of 1950s training, with the addition of fifty years of practice and personal evolution."

Master Harada, having thrown Steve Hope, follows up with an
excruciating pressure point attack to a nerve in the chest.

KDS, Sensei has become more 'personally' independent and self-confident outside the dojo."

During his time at the new flat, Master Harada returned to Japan once again for three weeks, after an absence of ten years, and was very disappointed with Karate practice. The students were as keen as ever, he said, but the old ways were disappearing, and all was sport orientated. Returning to Britain, he moved to South Wales where he now resides in a terraced two-bedroomed house, not alone as he has done for over thirty years, but with Marie Kellett, a 5th Dan student. *"He is happier now,"* says Marie.

The author asked Master Harada how he coped with the loneliness of all those years, spending so much time in and out of hotel rooms. Harada said that he got used to it, and if he ever felt lonely he would visit the local pub, and have one, but never more than two lagers. He would just sit there in a corner, not speaking to anyone really (he doesn't find small-talk easy), immersing himself in the atmosphere of others, and then go home. Ken Waight noted: *"When I looked at his life then* (mid to late Sixties) *it did seem rather a lonely existence. He often said the life of a teacher was lonely and told me not to be involved only in keiko. It was difficult teaching week in, week out, mostly with only students for company, whilst living alone in a country partly alien to him. I felt he led a lonely life, but his dedication, and perhaps his destiny, was to follow that path."*

Harada had an Alsatian, named Samurai, as a companion for a short while during the early Seventies, whilst living in Ealing (Master Harada loves animals), but he had to give him away because of all the travelling abroad. The part of Wales where he lives now is less noisy than London, and he likes the relative quiet, and being away from unnecessary distraction and obligation. He hopes one day to have another dog, a Great Dane, when the situation allows.

Readers may like to know that Master Harada, when at home, always takes a brisk daily walk for an hour or so, for additional aerobic fitness. Ziggy Boban once asked Master Harada why he lived in a top-floor flat. *"He said that the first thing that goes in the body when you get old is your legs, so it is important to keep them strong, for once they go you age rapidly. He would also wash his gi by placing them in a bowl and treading them as one treads wine. This, he said, helped keep his legs strong. Also the wringing-out process helped his grip and forearm muscles."* Practice is always on Master Harada's mind and, like his famous teachers before him, he never misses an opportunity to train.

Billy Haggerty, 5th Dan, a student of Master Harada for more than 20 years, remembers an incident that occurred at one hotel in Scotland in which Harada stayed. *"With Sensei coming to my home town so regularly, he got to know the managers and staff quite well, but as we spent so much time talking about Karate and practice, he rarely discussed any goings-on in the hotel. However, on one occasion, I was arranging a room for him when I bumped into the hotel manager, who inquired after Mr. Harada. He then said that it was very nice what Harada had done the last time he stayed there. I asked what he meant. The manager said that the last time Harada was there, a non-resident got drunk in the residents' lounge and when asked to leave, became violent, smashed a glass and tried to push it into the manager's face. At which point, Mr. Harada kicked the glass from the drunk's hand and apologised to the manager for the mess. The drunk was then easily restrained. Even after questioning, Sensei declined to talk about the incident."*

Perhaps a sign of the insular life Master Harada has led is his attachment to his books, of which he has many hundreds. *"He is lost without them,"* said Marie Kellett, and has substantial bookshelves, though far too many books for them, in his bedroom. Also, *"He is a very good cook,"* Marie acknowledges, *"especially noodle dishes and Japanese curries."* When the two of them visit London, they always stock up on particular foods and preparations. Atypically, for a Japanese, Master Harada also likes English food a lot, and is very fond of his Sunday lunch. He relaxes and watches old movies, especially detective and war films, but dislikes anything depressing as it makes him feel sad. Of an evening at home he will listen to his music. He has a wide taste, from the classics, especially Tchaikovsky, to opera, from military band marches to country and western. He also owns a karaoke machine, and plays a mean harmonica.

"Once," laughed Marie, *"his interests became too involved. He was accompanying a classic Japanese tune played on a karaoke machine in a bar in Tokyo with friends. At the same time he was watching, and got completely involved in, a samurai sword fight on the television in the bar, and fell behind with the words."* Few people, of course, see the other side of Master Harada, but he has, in Marie's own words, *"a good sense of humour,"* and is a genuine pleasure to be with. At home he is very quiet, reads a lot and, perhaps more than most people, dislikes domestic disruptions, or interference of any nature. Ziggy Boban and his wife once Spring-cleaned Master Harada's Ealing flat as a surprise for him. On returning from abroad, *"He didn't say anything,"* Ziggy recalled, and never offered the keys to his student again! Master Harada lives a simple life, and as long as he has a comfortable bed, food to eat, his Karate and his books (most of which are on Karate anyway), he is happy.

Billy Haggerty recalled two amusing stories. The first was when Master Harada had requested to visit Scotland, so that he could experience a typical New Year. *"So, in 1976, I arranged a hotel for him to stay at. He arrived on the night before New Year's Eve, quite late as I recall, and knowing that in Scotland there would be little rest over the next few days, I advised him to have a good night's sleep, which he promptly agreed to and I left him at his hotel. Next day I called in to his hotel to go for something to eat, and he did not look well. So I asked if something was wrong, and he just shook his head. Later, I discovered that there had been a private*

"Master Harada lives a simple life, and as long as he has a comfortable bed, food to eat, his Karate and his books (most of which are on Karate anyway), he is happy." A section of the Harada library, circa 1987.

The "naughty" photograph. Master Harada with Elizabeth Haggerty and her daughter, Jacqueline — 1982.

party in the hotel, and he had somehow got himself invited, and savoured Scottish hospitality until around five in the morning, with another five days and nights to go!

"On New Year's Eve, I took Sensei to meet my parents for the first time. My father offered him a drink. Still feeling the effects of the night before, Sensei tried to decline, but Hogmonay in Scotland is not a good time to go tee-total. My father never quite got his tongue around 'sensei', thinking that was his first name, and throughout the night called him 'Sensus'. As I took Sensei from one house to the next, the drinks didn't slow down until very early in the morning. By the time we reached his hotel the door was locked and we couldn't rouse the porter. I guess he got involved with the festivities as well. I *invited Sensei back to my flat, which was the only option available. There was only one bedroom, so I offered Sensei the bed and said I would get a sleeping-bag. But he insisted he would sleep on the floor and, being Japanese, would be quite comfortable. I don't think he was ready for the difference in temperature, as I found him huddled in front of the fire."*

The second story is, in many ways, a repeat of the Marta photograph incident, which the reader will, no doubt, recall. Billy Haggerty described the story so: *"After Harada Sensei had bought himself a full Highland Dress rig-out, he pulled me aside one evening and said, 'Billy, would it be possible for you to ask your wife to dress up with kilt, etc., and bring your baby so that I can have some photographs taken?' He didn't quite make it clear what he wanted to do, but it was obvious that he intended to joke with someone. So we set up the night and had several photographs taken, and we got Harada Sensei extra copies. Some months later, when we met Harada Sensei again, he gave us a beautiful baby's cape which had been hand-made and sent from Morocco. When we enquired as to whom it was from, or what it was for, he just laughed and said: 'They think I'm married. Even my mother thinks I'm married now.' Someone who saw the photograph wrote a letter to his mother on the subject. I pushed him further. 'What happened? What did you say?' And he said: 'The last time I was in France, there were several groups from different places and I showed them the photograph and said 'Well, sometimes a man makes a mistake.' And they drew their own conclusions from that.' I think he found this incredibly funny."*

Following the 1974 Summer School, Ziggy Boban remembers a humorous anecdote concerning Harada's views about women. Being invited, along with other senior KDS grades and their wives, to dinner at the Tokyo Restaurant in Swallow Street, London, the master made a number of tongue-in-cheek comments that stuck in Ziggy's mind. Boban continued: *"Sensei, during the conversation, said that he preferred men to women, because whilst a woman would make-up (make herself beautiful) for you, a man would die for you. Well we all shuffled around, leaving places vacant beside Sensei, whilst telling our female partners that we had limits to our loyalty. Sensei also suggested if he was to marry, his wife would have to be a mixture of all the world cultures. He would have a Welsh housekeeper, English nanny, French lover, Chinese cook, Italian mistress and a Japanese wife all rolled into one. We considered his two proposals and surmised that if he had this in mind, then it may have hindered his chances, hence he remained a bachelor!"*

When Master Harada worked for the bank, not all his superiors were supportive of his training, saying that he ought to concentrate on either banking or Karate. However, they were mostly well-meaning and he was often invited to dinners and barbecues to meet daughters and so on. Ziggy Boban tells a funny story about the master. *"In his attempt to be fashionable, he decided he should, like others, apply Brylcreem to his hair, but he didn't have any, so he used cooking oil/fat instead. While the visual effect was, at first, okay, he did have problems with the flies that became attracted to his hair, not to mention the problems when it got hot and the fat began to run!"*

On 3rd February 1986, the author had the pleasure of meeting Master Harada for the first time, when he was writing the book 'Conversations With Karate Masters' (the other masters featured were: Masafumi Shiomitsu [Wado-Ryu], Keinosuke Enoeda [Shotokan], Steve Arneil [Kyokushinkai] and Morio Higaonna [Goju-Ryu]). The near five-hour interview, which partly formed the basis of Chapter One of that book, was held at the master's Ealing flat. As the author has noted before, Master Harada has never sought the limelight. He has never been pushy, preferring to stay quietly in the background. This was one of the attributes that attracted the author to him. The book then allowed a new generation to become acquainted with the master and the Shotokai style, and opened-up further debate. The author is pleased to say that 'Conversations...', which was published in 1988 by Ronin Publishing ('Fighting Arts International'), was a great success.

Bey Logan, then Editor of 'Traditional Karate' magazine (Vol. 2 No. 5) wrote: *"The first master covered in the book is Harada Sensei. He is of particular interest to Karate students, as he actually trained under Gichin Funakoshi, though the latter was very old at the time. His memories of the great man are both honest and touching, and Harada himself is long overdue for a chance to air his views on the development of Karate in general."* If the truth were known, Harada had been largely forgotten outside his own circle. A means of expression had not arisen, and because of his nature and upbringing, Harada had not looked for it. As a consequence of the book he became, in the Karate world, much better-known, and further opportunities presented themselves.

In 1988 the Karate-Do Shotokai suffered a major split, and

Master Harada demonstrates on his student and companion,
Marie Kellett, 5th Dan.

the association halved its numbers to 500 students. This split had an upsetting effect upon Harada, a sensitive man. Losing senior grades was deeply hurtful after all the training and good times they had shared together. He had invested much emotional energy in them, in some cases in excess of 20 years, and had high hopes. Bitterly disappointed, he contemplated returning to Japan. But things picked up and he is much happier now. There is a positive feeling within the KDS, and Great Britain will remain his home. *"The British have a good spirit for martial arts,"* he said, *"as good as Japan".*

In 1990, the author's book, *'Mind Training For The Martial Arts'* was published. In Chapter Three, *The Art of Concentration*, the author elaborated upon an exercise (Exercise 12) that he had learned from Master Harada, and upon which he had written briefly earlier. The exercise is designed to overcome distractions and anxieties that invariably result in a confrontation situation, and takes into account what is known as broad concentration. One (unknown) critic wrote in his review (*'Traditional Karate'*, March 1991): *"There is also a real gem of an exercise from Mitsusuke Harada that alone is worth buying the book for"*. This was but one exercise, the truth is that Master Harada has a host of them.

As part of the Japan Festival held in Great Britain during 1991, the *Budo Sai*, or grand demonstration, was held at the Northumbria Centre, Washington, Tyne and Wear, just north of Durham, in September. As a festival to the martial arts, leading exponents from a number of arts were invited to demonstrate. Many of these teachers also held courses in Durham during that week. Aikido was represented by Yoshimitsu Yamada, 8th Dan, Takeji Tomita, 7th Dan, and Ichiro Shibata, 6th Dan; Kendo was represented by Hiroshi Ozawa and Masaru Minowa, both 7th Dan; Yuishinkai Kobudo (weaponry) was represented by Kishio Inoue, 7th Dan, Toshio Okabayashi, 6th Dan, and Julian Meade, 5th Dan; Wado-Ryu Karate by Masafumi Shiomitsu, 7th Dan, Toru Takamizawa and Yoshi Iwasaki, both 6th Dan; Goju-Ryu Karate by Morio Higaonna, 8th Dan, and George Andrews, 5th Dan; Shotokan Karate by Masao Kawazoe, 6th Dan, and some of his students, and Shotokai Karate by Mitsusuke Harada, 5th Dan and senior students. There was also a demonstration by Master Gato of Brazilian Capoeira, and a course in the Korean art of Taekwondo by Thomas Stammer, 4th Dan. The attendance at the

A demonstration of the kata 'Meikyo' at the 1991 Budo Sai.
"The British have a good spirit for martial arts, as good as Japan"
—Master Harada.

Three of the special guests and demonstrators at the 1991 Budo Sai.
Left to right: Master Morio Higaonna (Goju-Ryu Karate);
Master Takeji Tomita (Aikido) and Master Harada.

demonstrations was poor, however, despite widespread advertising.

Master Harada treated his demonstration and four-day course (held at the Meadowfield Sports Centre) with the seriousness that such a responsibility required. Unfortunately, like the demonstrations, the course was not well attended, with only some 20 students, for it followed Master Harada's Summer School and people were tired and had used up a substantial part of their annual holidays. I asked Master Harada whether he was disappointed by the low turn-out. He said that, *"Practice was okay. Even if only one person came, still practice."*

Tyne Tees Television spent five days at three different venues filming the events. The result was three 30-minute programmes involving two film crews, produced and directed by martial artist Ed. Skelding. The presenter for the series was martial artist and actor Terry O'Neill. Interviews and personal demonstrations for the programmes were held at a studio set up at the Abbey Leisure Centre, not far from the hotel where many of the masters were staying. This allowed for a controlled environment in order that correct lighting and so on could be utilised. First transmitted in the Tyne Tees area, Master Harada was featured in Programme Two, *'Finding The Way'*, which also featured Shotokan and Aikido. These are first-rate programmes, and the author would like to mention the accompanying music by composer John Cook as being particularly effective.

Master Harada's contribution began with O'Neill mentioning that Harada was the most senior Shotokai instructor in Europe. Then Master Harada performed his rendition of *'Meikyo'* (bright mirror), a deep and personal kata, advanced despite its seemingly straightforward moves and techniques. Introspection and sincere training over many years peel away the veil of illusion, and the master may look at his own reflection and see what truly is. For many practitioners, watching Harada's Shotokai for the first time, this was fascinating. More than a few eyebrows were raised no doubt, but one had to watch. Whereas typical Shotokan emphasises speed, dynamism of stance and power for example, Shotokai Karate-ka cultivate spirit and internal energy, giving their kata a very soft, relaxed and fluid, not to say seemingly powerless appearance. Note that the traditional *kiai* (focus of vital energy) points were not adhered-to in the kata. But the performance of *'Meikyo'*, although alien and confusing to many

*During an unrehearsed sparring demonstration at the 1991 Budo Sai,
Master Harada traps his opponent's (Marie Kellett) foot and delivers
a face punch!*

people, was well practised — of that there is no doubt. The opening sequence to the *joshin gamae*, before the first *gedan-barai*, is
a fine example of the Shotokai state of mind.

The kata demonstration was followed by one-step sparring
with Shotokai 5th Dan Marie Kellett. Master Harada defended
against *oi-zuki* (lunge punch) attacks using different blocks each
time and countering with such techniques as *gyaku-zuki* (reverse
punch), *uraken-uchi* (back-fist strike) and *shuto-uchi* (knife-hand
strike), and one throw. The display shown was simple and
effective. Then followed a one-minute unrehearsed freestyle
exhibition. Again with a complete lack of ostentatiousness, the
demonstration showed how Shotokai Karate-ka move continually to confuse and frustrate an opponent. The technique that
brought Harada's contribution to an end was when he pinned his
opponent's foot to the floor and countered to the face. This

raised a smile, a few chuckles, and applause. There was one final view of Master Harada, as the credits came up, which perhaps provides us with the best visual insight to the man and his style. He is pictured in the *kamae* guard. The author recommends that readers look at this closely — I shall say no more.

A report of events appeared in No. 72 of *'Fighting Arts International'* magazine. Entitled *The Masters and Methods of the Budo Sai*, Joseph Coop wrote the following of Master Harada, which sums-up the situation very well: *"Shotokai was represented by Mitsusuke Harada Sensei and his students. Their kata was such a contrast to the Shotokan that it hardly seemed possible that they had developed from the same source. Yet Harada Sensei was graded 5th Dan in Shotokan by the founder, Gichin Funakoshi. His style could not be more authentic. The Shotokan of Kawazoe relied on speed and focus, each technique supported by a strong, powerful stance, and his advanced kata, 'Kanku-sho' and 'Sochin', were determined and paced. In contrast, the kata of Shotokai were delivered by Harada at extraordinary speed, each technique being the immediate trigger for the next. The stances were short, light and the punches seemed unfocussed. I could not help wondering if I was watching a pageant of the history and development of Karate. Did the differences between the two examples, of what was basically the same style, reflect the changes in the physique and understanding between the generations?*

"Harada Sensei gave a demonstration of distance and timing in free sparring. He was able to avoid each attack with speed, control and ease, and at the end of each passage, entered his opponent's space to deliver a technique to a vital point. His stances were more upright and shorter than those used by Kawazoe Sensei. One point: I thought the punches were unfocussed and doubted their effectiveness, so I asked a Shotokai exponent to punch my stomach. I wish I had not been so foolish!"

The style certainly is deceptive. The lack of such mechanical movement characteristic, and often so impressive in Shotokan, is largely absent in the natural, reactive world of Shotokai practitioners. The problem that faces most Karate-ka watching Shotokai practice is, in this instance, the ill-advisable habit of comparison. The aims of the styles may ultimately be the same, but the mind set is different, so comparisons have little value. It is rather like two people journeying to an agreed point on the Equator, but one starts at the North Pole, the other at the South

On a black-belt course in Southampton in 1986, Steve Hope and Tony Lima demonstrate whilst Master Harada explains correct form.

Pole. Different experiences meet the travellers in different countries along the way, but they join hands at the end.

What came across in Harada's contribution was that he was confident, always in control, gentle, intimate, creative, one hundred per cent a teacher, giving rather than showing. Professor Mathieu expressed his opinion of Master Harada quite beautifully on one occasion, which seems appropriate here: *"He may be the greatest. The strongest doesn't mean much to me."*

Terry O'Neill in fact interviewed Master Harada, but it was not shown. This may be because, whilst Master Harada's level of English is very good, it takes a while to understand the diction and pronunciation, and clearly this would not have suited a television audience. Similarly, Harada demonstrated basics with a *bo*, but this wasn't included either. In fact, Master Harada had been on British television three times before, once in Birmingham around 1965, and twice in London. These had only been very short appearances though, and the *Budo Sai* gave him his first opportunity to be seen by a widespread audience in Great Britain.

Master Harada is no stranger to television, of course. As the reader may recall, he appeared on Brazilian television twice, featured on a short slot on Belgian television in 1963, and also in Monaco. He has graced the television screens in Morocco many times. Similarly, he has been interviewed in every country he has visited by newspaper journalists or editors and correspondents of martial arts magazines, and has appeared in a number of books in Japan, the most recent being in a commemorative edition marking the 60th anniversary of the Waseda Karate Club.

In November 1991, Master Harada travelled back to Tokyo for some three weeks, to take part in the celebrations to mark the above anniversary. The day started with speeches and demonstrations (from a number of countries) at the university dojo. Master Toshio Watanabe (Kamata), on one occasion, despite being in his seventies and dressed in a two-piece suit, led 40 or so students in *gi* in the kata *'Taikyoku Shodan'*. Master Watanabe is Chairman of Waseda University's 'old boys' group, and is a much-respected Karate-ka. He still practises Karate almost every day at the university, encouraging and giving guidance to the young students. The festivities continued with a superb buffet at a top Tokyo hotel. Many famous 'old boys' were present, including Akio Tsuruta, Hiroshi Kawaguchi, Hiroshi Noguchi and Tsutomu Ohshima.

Early in 1992, Master Harada wrote the foreword to the author's book *'Training With Funakoshi'*, which provided a synthesis of information about the famous Okinawan. Along with the aforementioned article, this foreword is all that Harada has written to date on Karate. This successful book helped to further establish him in the minds of '90s Karate-ka. Harada was also kind enough to supply original calligraphy by Master Funakoshi (*'Shoto'* and *'Funakoshi Gichin'*) reproduced in the book, and to provide the author with then-unpublished information.

From the late Sixties onward, Master Harada has taught widely in Europe. He currently visits France five times a year, Belgium once, Finland once, Morocco, Gibraltar and Portugal once or twice and is occasionally called-upon to instruct in other countries such as Sweden and Germany. When not abroad, as one might suspect, he teaches at the KDS dojos in England, Scotland and Wales, and runs a number of courses annually, some of which are open to trainees, regardless of style. His aim is to spread the true meaning of Karate-Do so that many may benefit from this noble, yet still generally poorly-understood martial art.

Seeking
The Way

"With him Karate is a never-ending obsession..." — an observation of Master Harada by Professor Mathieu.

Master Harada's enthusiasm for his art is boundless. The author remembers well spending some two hours talking to him about *kime* (focus), and practising different interpretations of it upon each other's stomach muscles in a Southampton hotel room, after his 29th successive British Summer School. In fact, Master Harada said he didn't really understand what *kime* was, and is unable to interpret the dictionary definition with any clarity. He drew a concrete distinction between explosive internal power and impact power gained from speed, weight, technique, emotional focus, and so on. Harada noted that different styles, and indeed different instructors practising in the same style, offer different definitions when pressed. Master Egami's explanation of *kime* was simply to knock someone down, Harada recalled, whereas others' definitions are often vague or overly comprehensive. For this reason then, Harada rarely refers to *kime* in his teaching. However, the discussion continued. *"This was how Egami used to punch." "This is how Yoshitaka used to strike the makiwara." "This is how Funakoshi Sensei used to grip."* Now that's privileged knowledge — and it's priceless. A few minutes later Master Harada's jumper, socks and shoes were off, his shirt sleeves rolled-up, and both watches were on the table. (Master Harada has the rather eccentric habit of wearing a watch on each wrist. The one on the left wrist is set to British time, the one on the right to European time.) *"This is how we block." "Punching here is strong,"* and the next second, *"How does Kanazawa teach keage* (snap-kick)? *I'm researching how Yoshitaka devised fudo-dachi."* Harada hadn't lost his love of Karate after 50 years, was still eager to learn from others, but perhaps most importantly of all, he wanted to share.

Professor Mathieu has noted that: *"Standing aside and letting things happen is simply something which he* (Harada) *can't do. I remember one day when in the course of one of his visits to Paris, we went to say hello to some of Ohshima Sensei's old boys. We had not meant to go to practice with them, but we dropped in at their dojo because we knew we would find them there, and he had a message to pass-on or a question to put to Daniel Shemla. As we arrived before the end of practice, we stood watching, but after about five minutes he was explaining some point to them…and in less than ten minutes he was on the tatami…forgetting about the time and everything else.*

"With him it (Karate) *is a never-ending obsession, but I can*

guarantee that we have great laughs on the way. I remember once, here in Rheims, we had been practising at the university gym with the students and of course, as usual, the class had gone on more than an hour over the official time, and the discussion had continued in the changing room between him, Jean Marie Dupont, my old-time partner and school-friend from Paris, and myself. While dressing he would then stop to show some point, and no matter how much or how little clothes we had on, he would have us training in whatever small space we had. Then we drove down to my place on the way back to his hotel, and I stopped for two minutes at my home to get something. When I came back to the car he had Jean Marie attacking him on the pavement while he demonstrated some point!"

In an interview with Arthur Lockyear (*'Fighting Arts International'*, No. 70), the famous Aikido master, Kazuo Chiba, already referred to in this book, described Harada as: *"An intellectual and a great Karate master"*. Certainly we can judge that Harada's Karate lineage is quite exceptional, and that he had dedicatedly pursued his art over six decades. Of course, the mind cannot be split from the body, and the thinking man uses his intellect to advance his Karate — to rise above the dogma that undoubtedly exists. Master Harada is a fine example of this, and a very rare one at that, for he is Japanese, and Japan's social conditioning system does not always lend itself to the questioning mind that Master Harada possesses.

"If a nail sticks up, knock it down" is a much-quoted Japanese dojo maxim. You are not only likely to find that maxim put readily into practice in dojos where an individual is arrogant, conceited and self-opinionated, but sometimes also where an individual threatens the established way of thinking — where he is perceived as rising above his pre-ordained station. Master Harada has lived in Japan for only 17 of his 65 years, and although those were formative, peer group pressure years, he couldn't wait to leave (though he still retains his Japanese passport). Such is the power of social conditioning that, even though Harada is well aware of the inherent weaknesses of the social system of the Japanese, and hasn't lived there for some 40 years, he still feels that it affects him greatly — but the ropes are not as tight as they might be!

Master Harada has made some important contributions to Karate. These carefully-thought-out and researched deliberations were dismissed out-of-hand when he went back to Japan. Even

Professor Mathieu's lunge-punch is abruptly stopped — Rheims, 1985.

though he was half-expecting such a response, the realisation that no-one was interested depressed him greatly, for he believed that he had something of genuine value to offer, but was met by a wall of resistance. Before we take a look at Master Harada's considerations, however, let us briefly survey his intellectual interests, for they have a bearing on the man and his development, and provide additional insight into his character and his Karate practice.

What Master Harada observes, what he reads, what he is exposed to, is considered and incorporated into his training. Bernard Mathieu recalled the many-a-long night, sometimes to the dawn, discussing the turn-of-the-century French philosopher Gaston Bachelard and the Greek Stoics. 'Stoics' was the name given to the followers of Zeno of Citium, who taught in Athens in the fourth and third centuries before Christ. They were uncompromising pantheists — who believed that God was present in all things. Master Harada's love of nature, in the widest sense, and all that it entails, is certainly exhibited in his Karate practice and teaching style — from the timing in his kata to the way he blocks, from the consideration of students inside the dojo to his interaction with non-practitioners outside the dojo.

The emotional wrenches that Harada went through in the questioning of fundamental practises in Karate was justified by linking-in with Gaston Bachelard's 'Philosophie du Non' (The Philosophy of Refusal). In his mind this provided a theoretical underpinning, gave an objective and logical response to the flaws that he saw in training, and combated the constraints that he had been brought-up with. Other interests include Buddhism and Zen, Henri Bergson's approach to Oriental philosophy and the work of the early 19th Century German idealist thinker, associated with the dialectic method of reasoning, George Hegel. In the field of economics, Master Harada is especially well-read on the work of the British economist John Maynard Keynes, who influenced economic thought all over the world, including post-war Japan. It is true to say that Master Harada has a refreshing and enquiring mind, which is often motivated by his students. For example, he studies Japanese and Chinese history because of the questions he is often asked by his more intelligent pupils — and if he doesn't know an answer he will find out. He teaches at dojos at the universities of Wales, Southampton, Durham and Rheims, and he finds it stimulating to converse with bright young minds, as they sometimes throw a new light, a different perspective, on an old problem.

But what of Master Harada's Karate and what he teaches? My first statement may confuse many readers when I say that Harada actually practices Shotokan Karate. Master Harada is quite insistent upon the point, as indeed he should be, and it is one that is certainly worth explaining. If you take any senior Karate-ka you will always find differences. These differences may be interpreted as being based upon perceptions and individual strengths, be they physical or psychological, inherent or learned. Each master has different interests, a different intellect, comes under different influences, and these are reflected in their practice. Master Kanazawa's Tai-Chi surely affects his Shotokan in a very positive way, for example. Master Higaonna's practice of striking a water-bag in preference to a punch-bag will be reflected in his style, and so on. Readers will recall that Funakoshi's death caused a split in his students. The Funakoshi family, along with selected senior grades, formed the Shotokai in order that the funeral might proceed in the prescribed manner. (To confuse matters, Funakoshi actually used the name Shotokai prior to this, but to

Master Harada demonstrates Tai Chi Chuan form.

elaborate upon the point is to get embroiled in Japanese Karate politics, which get deeply personal and are truly complicated!)

In 1957 there was really only one style of practice in the Way of Shoto, and that was referred to, of course, as Shotokan. When the name Shotokai was retained and an association formed there were, initially, no differences in style between those who had joined the new association and those who had not. It was only really in the mid-Sixties that significant changes began to appear, and these innovations were apparently the product of Karate-ka much junior to Master Harada, supposedly acting under the auspices of Master Egami. (Master Harada noted that if Egami had been allowed to train another ten years, Shotokai training would have been completely different.) As we have seen, Master Harada, after experimentation and unable to obtain a committed reply from Egami, essentially broke technical ties, and so reverted back to early 1950s training. With this training as a base, his form and practice, like all other senior grades, began to take on small yet inevitable changes as his own thoughts materialised physically. Unlike other Japanese masters, however, these changes became far more noticeable as he challenged even the most basic concept. Today, Master Harada noted, approximately 75 per cent of his practice is pure 1950s training, the remaining 25 per cent his own innovation, though the two are very closely intertwined. As one might imagine, such action did not exactly endear him to the establishment, and even now, after all these years, certain Japanese will not discuss particular issues with him.

The isolation that Master Harada has felt is no doubt reflected in his choice of art. Valuable parallels may be drawn. Readers may recall that the master felt an affinity with impressionism, fauvism and cubism. Interestingly, though perhaps the author should say inevitably, these movements were held in contempt, and their names were originally meant derisively. The impressionist exhibition of 1874 broke with tradition and was initially scorned by the establishment. However, their work led to the most important and influential movement of the 19th Century. Impressionism was based on the scientific study of light, and the play and reflection of light on objects using only the colours of the spectrum. Because of the ephemeral nature of their work, impressionist painters were fully conscious of change and the nature of change. The post-impressionist Paul Cezanne, the acknowledged father of modern art, was the strong influence

A side-step and throw demonstrated on Professor Mathieu.

behind cubism. Picasso and Braque, the most famous cubist painters, reduced forms to geometric shapes seen from a number of different angles. These different perspectives and planes were superimposed or criss-crossed to show that reality has, indeed, many faces. The Fauves, or 'wild beasts', a name applied as a result of the artists' bold and daring use of emotive colour, to express form and relief in a freely distorted manner, were frowned upon, yet Matisse was probably the most important artist this century. And, oh yes! Van Gogh. Of his hard and tortured life, Harada said: *"Very interesting"*.

Establishment art is limited. Creativity is dead. But conformity is tradition to the Japanese way of thinking, and it's a brave man who confronts it. Master Funakoshi did, and was heavily criticised back on Okinawa. Master Okuyama did, and was ostracised. Master Egami did, and was asked no longer to teach at a certain university. Master Harada did, and his seniors would not supply him with information. But these mavericks have contributed more in a few short years to Karate-Do than whole lifetimes by others who simply toed the party line, became establishment artists.

Readers may recall that the four basic elements of Harada's Karate in 1963 were: natural movement, correct form of posture, relaxation and concentration. These elements have not changed, but the manner in which they are defined and practised has undergone considerable revision. Each element is dependent on every other one and unless all four work in harmony, there is no true Karate. No ranking is therefore implied in their order. Let us now look at these elements more closely, initially though, in a round-about manner.

Master Harada recalled that, at university, the students could be roughly dichotomised into those who mostly practised hard at kata, and those who mostly practised hard at kumite. Harada noticed something of importance. When those who practised kumite stopped training and later returned, their style had deteriorated tremendously, whereas those who trained in kata kept their conditioning and could participate in sparring. *"This was very strange, and also very interesting,"* Harada commented. He remembers well a senior who had not trained in his usual kumite for some considerable time, coming up to him and saying: *"Harada, you are now very good."* Harada rather forcefully replied: *"No. It is you who are now very bad."* The senior knew this, and nodding his head, said: *"Now I understand what Funakoshi meant about the practice of kata".*

Master Harada has no objection to freestyle practice, indeed he engages in it himself, as we have seen from his willingness to 'put himself on the line' in unrehearsed kumite on television. But it certainly forms a relatively minor part of his practice and that of his students. Steve Hope remembers practising freestyle only after some 10 years of training, and Professor Mathieu, only after having gained his 2nd Dan. We are talking here of dojo freestyle, not sport Karate, not points. In Harada's Karate, there are no

*Master Harada side-steps Professor Mathieu's attack and counters with
tetsui-uchi (hammer fist strike).*

competitions, no getting excited over cheap trophies. Competition is not real, Harada said, the judges and referees don't take into account impact value, absorption, the true ineffectiveness of many techniques delivered in a sporting environment, and so on. Indeed, the KDS make a point of emphasising their commitment to not having competitions in recent, though rare, advertisements.

Master Harada said that one mustn't be fooled, for a lot of senior Karate-ka place great emphasis on kata because they can no longer perform kumite effectively. He remembers a Karate demonstration that he attended with his father whilst at university. The senior Karate-ka took precedence over their juniors, but these seniors rarely trained. A junior attacked his senior to the face with a lunge-punch during a sparring demonstration, and the senior inadvertently blocked to the stomach. The junior pulled his punch so as not to make contact, and the audience groaned. *"This is not Budo,"* his father said — and he was right. The audience saw it for what it was — a sham. *"These Karate-ka have no respect for their juniors or the audience,"* his father went on. The problem was not so much that the older Karate-ka did not want to train, but found that they could no longer practice in the same way that they had done 20 years earlier, due to their age — for that's really all the training there was at that time. Very few Karate-ka continued beyond the age of 40, Harada said. Additionally, the pressure put on employees by Japanese companies was immense and, in truth, the majority of the 'old boys' had little, if any time at all, to practice.

But Kendo was something different. Master Mochida, approaching 90 years of age, was attacked by a group of 7th Dan Kendoka at the same demonstration. *"No-one could touch him,"* Harada said admiringly, *"Forty, even fifty years his junior and they couldn't touch him. Why is that so?"* thought Harada, and after much consideration he came to the conclusion that it must be a question of the type of practice, and practice from the earliest stages. *" '————' is an outstanding Karate-ka, but he could have been much better if the original practice had been different,"* Harada said. *"But what is correct practice?"* Ueshiba had it in his late eighties, and age brings great Kendo and Judo masters *"whom everyone respects, but no-one in Karate has yet emerged"*. Harada continued: *"There is something fundamentally wrong with our practice,"* and he believes he knows what it is.

The reader may recall that Master Okuyama spent much time, reputedly, watching fish in the mountain streams during his two years in the mountains. According to Egami, Okuyama was of a higher level than Yoshitaka — and Egami would have known. The author would like to quote from his book, *'Training With Funakoshi'*, which has a bearing on this most important issue. It is a quote in which Master Harada shares the sentiment: *"The rhythm of the kata 'Niseshi', which became known as 'Nijushiho', is most interesting. The movements of this kata are said to follow the mood and currents in a river on its way to the sea, and the water's reaction to obstacles encountered on the journey. This is perhaps most evident in the opening sequence, though the feeling is strong throughout. Sometimes the moves are slow, deep and majestic — there are strong eddies. At other times we come upon powerful glides, swift white-water shallows, and even waterfalls. We encounter these things because we become one with the river. We enter the ki of the Way of Water. We can enter this system, for humans are composed of the same ki, the ki that pervades the universe. It is a case of looking beyond the form to capture the spirit. 'Nijushiho'*

Despite Professor Mathieu's substantial grip, Master Harada breaks his student's form.

represents a kind of pantheism in this respect, since it breaks down the artificial barriers between gods and men. When the mind is correct the technique is correct, but it takes many years for technique to flow. You will forget yourself — ego disappears, and time speeds on. Do I hear waves? Are they pine waves (as in 'Shoto') or water waves? No matter, there is no difference. Yes, we can learn much from practising 'Nijushiho'."

Each kata has its own rhythm, symbolises a scene from the natural world or an intent imposed by man. The translation of

'*Nijushiho*' is 'twenty-four steps' — an appallingly insensitive, bland and utilitarian name, completely inadequate to describe the kata's deep meaning. Similarly one asks why the name '*Gojushiho*' ('fifty-four steps') was chosen to replace '*Hotaku*', to describe Shotokan's most advanced kata? Funakoshi chose the name '*Hotaku*' so that students might appreciate the kata's affinity with the action of a woodpecker, not just its bill drilling into bark, but also the action of its wings and claws. Once the meaning of the kata is understood, everything changes, of which the timing is most noticeable. Master Funakoshi had a great love of nature and the rhythm of creation — he understood. Many others appear to have been locked in a spiritual void.

In his search for natural movement, Harada posed a question so simple that it is easy to overlook its significance. Expressed in an albeit rather elliptical way, he asked of a very senior Shotokan master: "*Why cannot ——————— use his Karate in his golf?*" The Japanese response was: "*Golf is golf, Karate is Budo — they are completely different*". But are they? Harada argues, are they really? It is a serious problem that needs to be addressed. To Master Harada's way of thinking, the Japanese response proved to be badly flawed and riddled with inconsistency. Harada believes the effects of Karate training should shine through in all walks of life by tapping into this natural flow and thus gaining benefit. Karate-Do is, in his mind, no less than a reflection of life itself, and much about being human is hidden, suppressed, denied expression. Whether it is the swing of a club to the catching of a ball, the essence should be discernable. But there is another point also. The swing of the golf club is performed in a flowing manner at its most refined, the catch gives, the tennis racket plays through, and so on — why then are 'traditional' Karate techniques so different? Why are punches, for example, delivered so abruptly? Once this is corrected, as Master Egami found, we are in another league altogether, and much that is deemed good form in 'traditional' Shotokan is, in fact, unnatural, weak and self-defeating. However, such 'traditional' techniques give the appearance of being strong and potentially devastating, and therein lies their attraction and appeal. Really powerful techniques paradoxically look soft and relatively weak. Acquiring such technique takes many years of dedicated training. There are no shortcuts — no masters in less than 20 years.

"*The question of natural movement means not being stiff, rigid,*

*All a question of timing. Master Harada stops Professor Mathieu's
advancing attack with a punch to the chest — Reims, 1986.*

regimented and closed in mind and body," Harada said. Yoshitaka
Funakoshi was in the right direction, but died. Egami was in the
right direction but became too ill to practice. Okuyama left
Karate for a branch of Aikido where the flow is easier to discern.
In those intervening 40 years little had changed in mainstream
Karate. There has been no significant evolution, and Funakoshi's
earnest wish of continued development after his death has not
materialised. The only noticeable thing that has happened is that
Karate has become popular throughout the world, and as a consequence has sunk largely to gymnastics and sport.

The problem of stagnation gives rise to four broad and

reasonable possibilities. Firstly, as an art, Karate-Do is so close to perfection that little needs to be changed. Secondly, that errors exist but no-one is capable of divining them. Thirdly, there are considerable errors that senior grades are aware of but are not prepared to challenge, and fourthly, there are errors that senior grades are aware of and which a few of them confront. The answer to our problem is best served if we examine Harada's challenge to quite fundamental concepts. His objective is simple — to devise a method of practice that will last a lifetime, so that a Karate master in his nineties can genuinely better men much more than half-a-century his junior, and that the journey is progressive, self-actualising and offers something of deep moral and spiritual value. This, Harada believes, may well give rise to the acquisition of a special kind of power — a power that Morihei Ueshiba supposedly possessed.

But this power comes from a lifetime of correct practice, and if access to such practice is unavailable, then it is not surprising that Karate is often seen as a poor relation to Aikido and Kendo, for example. Master Funakoshi did not display this special power that Master Harada speaks of, and so people questioned Karate. To put it simply, this special power involves influencing opponents' actions without touching them. Stories of Master Ueshiba throwing opponents without physical contact abound, and the reader may recall that Master Harada saw this twice. *"It is a metaphysical concept of Budo. How to do this physically is my challenge,"* Harada said. *"To find the true common denominator (where all Ways meet) and apply it to Karate, this is what I search for — to find it is my ambition"*.

It was because Master Egami suggested that Harada search for this elusive ability in Karate that he deliberately avoided the study of Shinwa Taido. The author asked Master Harada if he believed the stories associated with the revered master warrior Yamaoka Tesshu (1837-1888). An enlightened swordsman and founder of the intense Kendo style known as Itto Shoden Muto-Ryu (School of No-Sword), Tesshu insisted that no-sword swordsmanship was ultimately true spirit. It is said he could make bruises appear on his students' bodies by merely pointing his sword at them. *"Yes, I do believe. I really do believe,"* Harada replied sincerely.

It is interesting to note that Master Harada has actually practised with the *bokuto* (like a *bokken*) for over 20 years, and indeed

Master Harada places great value in bokken (wooden sword) and bo (staff) training for Karate-ka: here he demonstrates a bo technique on Tony Lima, 5th Dan.

The Master uses his foot (and split-second timing) to stop Marie Kellett's attack, during a 1970 course in Gibraltar.

his *bokuto* has almost become part of him. Ziggy Boban tells a story set at a midnight practice session during a Summer School at Warwick University. In the darkness, Master Harada asked someone to get his *bokuto*. When the student returned with the weapon, Harada said that it was not his. *"Well, we were all amazed as we could not even see the person next to us...Eventually the right one was found, the demonstration was carried out in silence, apart from the swish of the wooden sword and the sharp intake of breath of the assailant, who later confirmed that the bokuto had glanced down his tunic. Sensei told us that he knew the first bokuto was wrong, not by grip or weight, it just didn't 'feel' right."*

Master Harada's *suburi* (sword-cutting motion) had been faulted by Master Tamura (the two share a mutual interest in pedagogy), and Harada asked Master Chiba to show him how to perform the downward motion correctly. Master Harada places great value in *bokken* (and *bo*) training for Karate-ka, as it encourages correct use of the hips, aids centring, helps focus the exhalation, and generally develops the martial spirit. He also believes that the 'special power' comes with its practice. Yoshitaka and Master Okuyama used the motion, without the sword, to palm off opponents with great power. The author would equate it with practising *age-zuki* (rising punch) with a weight. When the weight is removed, the technique (if performed correctly) is fast, very light and relaxed, appears and feels soft, and is extremely powerful. The feeling produced is what advanced Karate technique should feel like all the time. but this is only the first stage, of course. What is important, however, is that with much practice, this feeling is internalised having, in Harada's words, *"created the correct body structure"*.

Later, Harada considers it is possible to project the results of the feeling onto an opponent, hence his belief in the stories surrounding Tesshu. At a psychological level, it is as though one focuses on the point of the *bokken* during practice, but when the *bokken* is removed, the mind still concentrates upon that point, and the effects are as if the weapon remained. It is no less than the mental projection of a feeling, of intent, that has real consequences in the physical world. Master Egami was *"very interested in this intellectually,"* Harada said, but was convinced that Ueshiba was the only one living (then) to have mastered it. Egami spoke of harnessing the flow of vital energy or *ki*, the fundamental element of the universe from which all things are

Master Harada engages in bokken practice with Master Takashi Kiyooka. Both wore white hakama in this 1969 photo.

composed, and focusing them with practice. Certainly, Master Ueshiba believed that he had acquired some special kind of *ki*.

Intriguingly, Harada said that this power is around us all the time, but it hasn't been analysed, for we have not recognised it for what it really is. In basketball and rugby it happens occasionally, he said. You will see a player in pursuit of an opposing player with the ball, come close and then, suddenly, when confrontation seems inevitable, quite inexplicably fall down. But how to tap this, and channel it in Karate, where self-suggestion is removed? *"It will only happen when the attacker is giving one hundred per cent,"* Master Harada confidently reported, *"and this is Karate's weakest point"* (as far as studying the phenomena is concerned). The rarity and indeed awareness of complete attacks in training currently prevents understanding and reliable scientific testing.

In order for natural movement to be recognised and then tapped, students need to create the correct body structure. If one is able to achieve this through hard practice, then as one gets older and youthfulness is lost, the vitality remains. The question is, of course, how best to prepare for this effectively? Master Harada has thought long and hard on this subject. The body needs to be trained in a repetitious nature, left and right sides, so that it becomes conditioned. But rather than opposing an opponent, from the first lesson onward students are taught body language and perceptivity through a number of simple exercises. The exercise already mentioned in the previous chapter is a good example, whereby constant practice, moving, keeping the correct distance, finely tunes the body to subtle shifts of one's opponent. The end result being that one moves in accord with one's opponent, like a shoal of fish or a flock of birds — together. As the simple movements are practised, the mind and body become desensitised of fear of an opponent, and one learns to respond naturally, to enter one's opponent's energy flow. It is important to 'keep the structure', because that is a constant, a bearing from which others' actions may be judged and one's own progression made observable. Working with an opponent like this is analogous to working with the *bokken* in a psychological sense, as long as the correct distance between partners is adhered to.

The draining-away of physical tension and mental anxiety through familiarity gives rise to that most valuable of commodities — relaxation, which, of course, in turn provides greater

Master Harada demonstrates a potential take-down against Professor Mathieu's lunge-punch.

freedom of mobility and more natural movement. Physically, the stances become less strained, undue tension does not lie in the body and particularly the joints, and the air is one of softness and naturalness that belies the power of the resultant training. The muscles are given a plentiful supply of oxygen which warms them and carries away waste products such as lactic acid. Mental relaxation means relaxed attentiveness, not having an empty mind, but a clear mind, that may respond to any situation. Brain wave patterns change from beta to alpha and even theta waves — moving Zen, the real thing.

Natural, relaxed movement, with the correct mind, means the acquisition of elusive 'heavy' techniques. Billy Haggerty recalled: *"Harada Sensei had been describing how to use heavy hands as a means of power and one individual was explaining that he was having a great deal of difficulty in understanding this, at which point he then asked if Sensei had any exercises which would allow him to understand this. Harada Sensei promptly replied: 'Yes. Come over toward the wall bars.' He then removed the person's belt and tied his hands at a tiptoe stretch to the wall bars. The person was then left there for the remainder of the two-hour session, and just before we completed the session someone reminded Harada Sensei that he was there. He got someone to untie the belt…(instructed the student to) continue to hold his arms up. He then got someone else to attack and, at a given command from Sensei, the person holding the belt was instructed to release it. The arm dropped rapidly, knocking away the strike with ease. Harada Sensei concluded: 'This is heavy hand'."*

Another incident occurred when Haggerty, having broken his wrist, went to the dojo with his arm in plaster to watch the class. Master Harada came over and asked why he wasn't training, so Haggerty raised the plastered wrist. Harada's immediate reaction was: *"What's wrong with your other hand? This would be a great time to learn something else."* Haggerty hadn't brought his *gi*, but Harada instructed another student to get him a spare. Haggerty continued: *"I had recently purchased a Japanese katana and as Harada Sensei had intended to use it on this particular course, I had brought the sword with me. When Sensei realised I had the sword, he immediately brought it out, unsheathed it, and had me hold both arms outstretched with one hand holding the sword and the other hand holding up the newly-fitted plaster cast, as a means of developing strength in my upper arms."*

In kata, the opponent is removed, but there is a projection of self-confidence and a strong visualisation of an adversary is drawn-up from intellectual and emotional reserves. There is just you and space. This is one form of mind training. The techniques flow naturally. Master Harada's kata are taught often at great speed to enhance conditioning, at other times very slowly. Time is stretched, analysis is possible initially (later time absorbs the attention) and so the practitioner becomes aware of his form.

At the physical level, Master Harada gradually analysed the whole body structure to determine what happened during events. He consulted doctors, sports coaches, studied bio-mechanics, muscular chains, and so on, always questioning what he was doing, never entirely satisfied — The Philosophy of Refusal, dismissing the irrelevant and disregarding established constraints. The result was an improvement in speed, freedom of mobility, finer timing, better distancing, greater speed upon impact, and so on. By questioning, the master's Karate evolved, and continues to evolve. Parting the clouds, seeking the Way — *Hatsuun Jindo*.

Master Harada demonstrates the value of a strong stance.

"O'Sensei (Funakoshi) *just taught kata, fixed form*," Harada said, "*not related to the real world*". Everybody was required to do the same thing at the same time — there was no consideration for the individual. Master Funakoshi was a classic example of a 19th Century Japanese schoolmaster, and he 'inflicted' his schoolmaster's approach, which he had used to teach kata to children, on the university system. Whilst this provided a very sound method of social conditioning and good internal discipline, one may argue, it did not necessarily augur well for the development of Karate as a Way. Master Harada said that the original Okinawan method of training was more informal and individually based, with students building upon their own development. Readers may already be aware that Master Funakoshi believed that he was Master Azato's only student. In real self-defence situations, forms are often very far from appropriate. Work with Capoeiristas, Aikidoka and boxers made Harada only-too-aware of the strict limitations of Funakoshi's Karate as a genuine form of self-defence — indeed it was more a case of wishful thinking.

True Karate relies on the harmony of mind and body through correct breathing (*kokyu*) and this is paramount in Master

Master Harada and Professor Mathieu demonstrate a training method designed to enhance correct posture for mae-geri (front kick)...

Harada's training. He insists that the medium be understood for, as Master Ueshiba noted: *"Aikido begins and ends with kokyu"* (*'Aikido: The Way of Harmony'*, J. Stevens, Shambhala: 1984), and traditional Karate is no different. Master Egami wrote that *"although we read about breathing...(it is) not discussed, perhaps out of shame of our ignorance"* (*'The Heart of Karate-Do'*, Kodansha: 1980). One harnesses mind and body through *kokyu* and *ki* becomes accessible. Master Egami noted — in the same

... the kick is delivered! Both photos were taken during a course in Brussels in December 1993.

book — that we should *"learn the power that nature has endowed us with and how to use it, for a man has a great deal of hidden power of which he is not aware"*.

Breathing is the key. In the traditional ways, inhaling and exhaling is viewed as a means of entering the rhythm of life, and is quite unlike the chest-orientated mechanical breathing people tend to use in their frenetic and stress-bound daily lives. Master Harada will sit for a lengthy period, back straight, relaxed, inflating the abdomen slowly whilst inhaling and slowly contracting the abdominal muscles as he exhales. This method of breathing is quite natural, and is observable in infants, animals and usually adults when they are deeply relaxed or asleep. Exhaling always takes considerably longer, of course, and one should aim for perhaps two inhalations/exhalations per minute, though nothing should be strained. Because the mind is apt to wander, Master Harada asks students to count (in their mind's voice — no sound should be made). By internally counting "One...", and holding the 'n' sound as one exhales, rather like chanting a monosyllabic Buddhist prayer (if such a thing exists), the mind concentrates on breathing with minimal distraction. Master Harada may practice this one or two hundred times each sitting, though later, of course, one may drop the internal count as one is able to concentrate on the breathing alone.

Breathing formed the basis of Billy Haggerty's "*most memorable incident with Harada Sensei*" in over twenty years. "*In those days we would spend five hours, non-stop, often practising things like fast Sambon kumite...At that particular time we were encouraged to continue attacking even when our partner could not defend against our attack. This sharpened our reactions and encouraged us to do well to avoid being hit. As myself and someone else were practising intently like this over the weekend* (course), *Harada Sensei was constantly coaching one side, then the other, and as one of his main points he kept declaring 'Breathe out! Breathe out!' It seemed no matter which point in time Sensei came toward us, he would still repeat 'Breathe out!' After extensive hard practice we constantly wanted to breathe in, rather than out all the time. It became clear that there was obviously some misunderstanding between us and on one occasion when he came over, we stopped and asked: 'Sensei, when do we breathe in?' To which he replied, 'Anytime. It doesn't matter when you breathe in as long as your body condition is one of breathing out'. We pushed him a little further on this topic because we found it difficult to understand what he meant. At this point he stopped the class, brought everyone together and went into a series of demonstrations where sometimes he would breathe in while defending, sometimes he would breathe out while defending, but each time emphasising that his body condition had remained the same — in a condition as though breathing out.*"

In traditional Karate we inhale through the nose to benefit health. The hair-like projections, called cilia, trap particles and

A low kicking attack by Master Harada at a Summer School in 1985

bacteria which would otherwise enter the lungs directly, causing all kinds of possible problems. As air passes through the nasal cavity it is warmed by blood vessels close to the skin surface and mucus in the nose keeps the air moist. Breathing dirty, cold and dry air in through the mouth is a habit to be discouraged generally, for not only can it be a possible aggravated cause of dental decay, but also, as the air has not been prepared to be accepted by the lungs, is a recipe for throat and bronchial complaints. Abdominal breathing aids stability and centring, with a subsequent increase in speed and power. When the air is sharply exhaled through the mouth, which is the most direct route, the greatest volume of air is expelled in the shortest possible time, which, of course, aids the focussing of techniques. Such breathing can not only alter body shape, but can also change the way we think and even our character if practised correctly over many years.

True Karate training does not require much muscle at all to be highly effective, but particular muscles are built-up through correct practice. The abdominal muscles are particularly important with regard to Karate training, as correct form centres around the *hara* and hips. The arms and legs are seen as relaxed extensions of the *hara* and hips. A Japanese will say "*hara wo neru,*" that he is training his stomach. With correct abdominal breathing the muscles of that region will unite with the wishes of the mind, producing a beneficial union and great power.

Here seems a good point to return to Master Harada's paper-punching practice, and the '*koan*' Master Okuyama set him. Ziggy Boban recalled when he visited Master Harada's Ealing flat in 1982, "*I saw that Sensei had hung a bulldog clip from the ceiling. When I asked what it was for, he told me: 'Well, you put some paper in the clip and then practice gyaku-zuki against the paper, the aim being to pierce the paper with your fist.' He said you really had to concentrate on a spot on the sheet of paper, and the 'Sun' newspaper was particularly good for that. So he showed me, and sure enough, within a couple of attempts, his fist pierced the paper without ripping it. I tried, to no avail, consoling myself in the fact that we had no copies of the 'Sun' to use.*"

Sometimes, Harada's quest for understanding can take on potentially extreme perspectives. Steve Hope remembered a situation which arose at a Summer School at Grange Farm that gives a very real indication of what Master Harada was prepared to suffer in his search. They were training at six o'clock in the morning, and an Indian religious group was watching. Some of the older members of the religious sect approached Sensei and said: "*We have our own martial art. We can kill with one punch.*" Harada said: "*Very interesting, please show.*" "*No! No!*"...(one of the sect said)... "*I will kill you.*" Harada replied: "*It doesn't matter if you kill me. This case I have witnesses. This case I asked, so no problem.*" The Indians went away untested. Professor Mathieu entered the conversation. "*This has happened a number of times. These so-called 'killers' live in fanciful dreams and try to impress people with wild statements they can never substantiate. I've had the same statements made to me but never found any of their attacks worth mentioning when put to the test."*

Master Harada works very hard thinking of new strategies, based on his research, to improve his students, to allow them to develop in their own way, in the structured framework, the discipline, whose parameters we call Karate-Do. How best to relay the information so that it will appeal to the different types of personality that make up any Karate association, is a problem that is always on his mind. *"Karate is like a computer. Human beings are like computers. We must find better software. We must keep the roots, be aware of what happened in the past and progress."* He went on to say that because of the stifling Japanese system, Japanese Karate-ka don't ask any questions. Europeans, on the other hand, ask questions all the time, and this is why, in many ways, European Karate is more advanced than that of Japan. He always walks a narrow path, however, in the sense that it is his mission in life to pass on what he considers to be true Karate and expects his students, especially his senior grades, to work with dedication

On the other hand, at the back of his mind is an incident that occurred during his middle school days. A close friend wanted to enter the Merchant Navy but suffered from colour-blindness. A teacher at the preparatory school encouraged him all the way, insisting that his student work very hard to gain entry, despite knowing that he would never be allowed owing to his disability. When Harada's friend was inevitably refused entry, he promptly committed suicide. Master Harada, learning from this unfortunate and extreme experience, never gives false hope to his students, but is always reassuring and full of encouragement after asserting the truth openly.

Before teaching a class, Master Harada noted that it is important to remove mental pressure. An hour or so before he leaves to train, he said he tries to relax completely. Sometimes he will simply sit down, though normally he will lie down or take a warm bath. When lying down, Master Harada will assume the Corpse Pose or *Savasana* of Yoga. He will enter his deep breathing mode already mentioned, which brings him into close contact with his body. During this quiet time alone, he will, in his relaxed state, practice the visualisation and mental rehearsal of kata, which Master Harada called 'super learning'. The techniques of visualisation are certainly to be highly recommended, and are addressed in Chapter Two, *The Power of Mental Imagery*, of the author's book *'Mind Training For the Martial Arts'*, which gives some practical exercises readers might like to try (the book also has exercises to encourage relaxation and concentration).

"Kata are very important," Harada said. They strengthen the body, condition the mind, train the spirit, enhance co-ordination and rhythm, improve the reflexes and allow a contact with the past. They are the essence of Karate-Do. The kata he teaches are: *'Taikyoku Shodan'*, *'Taikyoku Nidan'*, *'Taikyoku Sandan'*, *'Heian Shodan'*, *'Heian Nidan'*, *'Heian Sandan'*, *'Heian Yondan'*, *'Heian Godan'*, *'Tekki Shodan'*, *'Tekki Nidan'*, *'Tekki Sandan'*, *'Bassai Dai'*, *'Bassai Sho'*, *'Kanku Dai'*, *'Kanku Sho'*, *'Jihon'*, *'Jitte'*, *'Jiin'*, *'Enpi'* (*'Empi'*), *'Gankaku'*, *'Hangetsu'*, *'Sochin'*, *'Nijushiho'*, *'Meikyo'*, the Goju-Ryu kata *'Sanchin'* and *'Tensho'*, and the *bo* kata *'Matsukaze'*, which was created by Yoshitaka Funakoshi.

The JKA Shotokan kata that Harada does not teach are therefore: *'Chinte'*, *'Unsu'*, *'Wankan'*, *'Gojushiho Dai'* and *'Gojushiho Sho'*. Experienced Karate-ka might like to know that Master Harada never speaks of *bunkai* but *bunseki*. He explained that *bunkai*, the application of kata moves, means to break-up, then re-assemble, re-insert, which he described as a negative analysis. This might be compared to studying an amputated finger, then an amputated toe and trying to study what makes them work, or putting a line around a figure in a painting. *Bunseki*, on the other hand, takes the living kata (as it were) and infers how sections work but not in isolation to one another — rather like a pointillist painting, where coloured dots merge to form a picture which is observable only when one stands back. This gives meaning to the maxim that 'the whole is greater than the sum of its parts', and kata are a fine example of this. Master Harada described *bunseki* as positive analysis. An esoteric point maybe but it is important, and will give the reader some idea of the depth of thinking and exactness that Master Harada employs in his Karate.

So, what does all this theory amount to? What is it actually like to partner Master Harada? Steve Hope noted: *"To practice with Harada one to one on a personal basis is the ambition of most seniors in the Shotokai. To me it is practice experience without equal."* Let us then allow some of Harada's senior students to say a few words on the matter.

Roy Margetts, a 210lb. 4th Dan Karate-ka, describes his first

Master Harada explains a point whilst sitting in seiza, during a Summer School held in Canterbury in 1990.

encounter with Master Harada's 'soft' style, and what the experience gave him, so: *"I had been training with Karate-Do Shotokai for a number of years and attended numerous weekend courses, plus a few summer camps under Sensei Harada's instruction but I had yet to engage Sensei in 'personal practice' (i.e. partner him).*

"Sensei Harada was staying in Wales, between two consecutive weekend courses, and was teaching at local club venues during the week. On one of these evenings Sensei called me over and requested that I attack him with gyaku-zuki (reverse punch). I am quite stocky and have always considered my punch to be reasonably strong — some local higher Dan grades had been having major problems trying to defend against it. I took my posture to attack...(and) attacked. Sensei defended with gedan-barai and knocked me over. This was repeated several times. Sensei then requested I attack with oi-zuki (lunge punch). I did. His subsequent defence took me clean

out of my posture and knocked me over. Next I was asked to make a three-stage attack (Sanbon kumite) with oi-zuki to the head at speed. Sensei defended with age-uke (rising block) *and the results were the same as before, sometimes taking me out on the first attack, sometimes the third, etc., each time sending me flying all over the dojo.*

"*Sensei was always in complete control and seemed indifferent to a 95-kilogram mad Welshman 30 years his junior trying to knock his head off!*" (Roy Margetts later added that "*At all times when Sensei was knocking me over, he never hurt me. He just used correct technique applied with impeccable timing.*") Margetts continued: "*Most people would have been satisfied with the result, but Sensei went on to explain the weak point he was picking up in my attack which made it relatively easy for him to defend against me. He explained that my shoulders were a little too stiff, which was giving indication of the attack, also making it easy to break my posture and balance, when he defended. He went on to explain by giving a physical example of my problem. Firstly, he attacked oi-zuki to my chest. With some shoulder tension this caused some pain but it was only superficial, a surface pain. He then demonstrated his oi-zuki. This was completely different, no surface pain but a deep internal pain, almost sickening* (I must add Sensei was controlling his attack). *By pointing out one of my weak areas, Sensei gave me a new challenge. To improve my attack, make it stronger, quicker. This in future would mean Sensei would have to work harder when we next practised together. Harada Sensei creates this with all his people. He creates strong partners which make strong demands on his ability, which keeps his level very high. He never compromises, he always expects maximum effort from his people.*"

Steve Hope remarked that: "*On a course in Jersey, when I was in my mid-thirties, and with nearly 20 years of practice experience, I was lucky to be able to practice with Sensei for two-and-a-half hours each day for three consecutive days. I would attack him with all my might, but each time I would find myself on the floor, my attack broken.*"

And, Tony Lima, 5th Dan: "*He* (Harada) *would call me over on a training session and practice with me personally for two hours at a stretch. This would take the form of me attacking him with either gyaku-zuki, oi-zuki or mae-geri. He would accept my attack each time with the unavoidable result of me being sent flying to the floor some six to ten feet away! In a typical two-hour session with him I*

Master Harada performs a dangerous side-step against a front-kick to the head from Professor Mathieu — Rheims, 1985.

would probably attack him 100 times and hit the deck the same number of times! There were no words exchanged, only grunts and groans from myself, laughter from Sensei, and a thanks and a hand-shake at the end of the session."

Tony Lima continued: *"One particular session that I remember well was attacking him for two hours with mae-geri jodan (front kick to the head) at Southampton University. Each time I attacked him he would side-step, check my knee with his hand and fumikomi (stamp kick) my supporting leg. Eventually this taught me to strengthen my supporting leg, thus gaining stability, and increase the speed of my kick. Toward the end of the session my kicking speed and co-ordination had improved, so that at one stage my foot must have been about two inches away from his face. Just as I was about to taste sweet victory, he dropped on his back and at the same time swept away my supporting leg with one of his feet and placing the other on my stomach, thus sending me somersaulting over him to land in a heap!...Such was my practice relationship with Sensei that I had only one objective in mind...to knock him down. Each time I met him, I would say to myself: 'Okay, today you are going down'. Although I (always) wound-up flat on my back I was totally satisfied for I had given him my best on each attack. Needless to say I later understood that this is the essence of real practice. Without real, meaningful attacks, Karate cannot exist. Real practice means creating the situation/environment where one can attack seriously without fear of upsetting the partner. Easy to say, hard to do! Through my practice with Sensei, I have understood this physically and I am now able to reproduce a similar environment with other black-belts. This Sensei has given me, a unique tool, how to create good quality partners, and in so doing create and develop oneself."*

As Professor Mathieu noted: "*He takes enormous risks, and one episode…in Morocco he asked me to attack him with a bo. That was a time when he was practising distance. Instead of stepping back on the attack with the bo, he was stepping forward…As usual I was translating, explaining the points to the Moroccans. I had the heavy bo which I use all the time, and I know that to practice properly you have to give everything you have, otherwise, if you hesitate maybe, timing and direction are affected, and this is when you have accidents. He scared the life out of me, because I knew that I was going full power, and if he'd missed I thought I'd break his skull no problem, and he came to the point where the bo just touched his gi…Then he stopped and said to me: 'Why aren't you explaining?' I said: 'Sensei, I can't even talk…I'm so scared.' I was going full blast at him.*"

"*When I attacked Sensei with the bokken,*" said Steve Hope, "*as I started the swing down onto his head, his bokken would sweep smoothly down and sometimes put a red mark down my chest and stomach, or make a noise as it hit my gi. On occasions, Sensei would ask me to attack him with a live blade. In these instances I confess I was more concerned for myself than Sensei.*" And attacking with a knife, "*There was no holding back as the point would be lost, and anyway, Sensei would only get annoyed. In attacking, I usually ended up being thrown or knocked across the dojo floor. To let go of the knife as I was thrown was, of course, dangerous to the people watching, so I had to make sure I held on to the weapon without injuring myself. It seemed at times that it would be easier to catch my own shadow than to catch Sensei…And mae-geri? Many times I've touched him on the chin with a front kick. In this case if you have been practising maybe for three-quarters of an hour, the adrenaline is running, you tend to forget yourself, you really attack, you really*

Master Harada stops an attack without touching his opponent... in the air is Steve Hope, a 5th Dan from Southampton.

forget all circumstances. In this case you really let go." Such a case was in Finland, *"I attacked with mae-geri to the throat. Sensei moved smoothly out of my distance where he paused for a split second, so that my toes brushed his chin, such was his control."* Professor Mathieu noted, however, that: *"...there are times, of course, like anybody else, when he fails. I've seen his arm from here to there...as black as coal."*

It is not surprising, then, after such an evening's training, when Master Harada may literally put his life on the line, that the adrenalin is coursing through the master's body to the extent that he cannot sleep for a long time afterwards. He will often sit up in the small hours, reading — no guessing what about! Master Harada went on to say that teaching is very tiring. When abroad, especially when he has consecutive weeks in Finland and then

Morocco, meal times go out of routine and the body's circadian rhythms are jarred. When he returns home, he is exhausted and needs a week to fully recover. It is surely a sign also, given his age, of the effort he puts in.

But how far has Master Harada travelled, and how close is he to realising his goal of, in his own words, "*paralysing from a distance*"? Well, a number of his senior grades believe he has now achieved this. As Tony Lima put it: "*Many martial artists have read in books how masters such as Tesshu or Ueshiba knocked people over without touching them. I do not have to try to imagine or figure how this might have felt to the attacker. Thanks to Harada Sensei I have experienced this personally on many occasions whilst practising with him.*" Tony Lima was so impressed with Master Harada that, as a 1st Dan, he left his home in Gibraltar in 1979 and came to England to follow his teachings. He has since assisted the master in many countries.

Matters may not be quite as astonishing as they first appear, however. Is Master Harada able to immobilise, or throw opponents without making contact? This question was answered and nicely expressed by Billy Haggerty, now Chief Instructor to Shoto Budo, in a '*Fighting Arts International*' interview (No. 81) with 4th Dan Stephen Murray: "*It is true, yes. However, there is nothing mystical about this, nor did Sensei ever claim that there was. I personally can also knock someone down without touching, but it would be entirely wrong to suggest that I can knock anyone down without touching them. There is a situation whereby, when you have been struck, you remember the experience, and naturally you don't like it. So, the unconscious mind is always trying to look after you. For example, if someone hands you a red-hot poker and asks you to hold it by the hot end, the unconscious mind, that is of the average thinking person, stops you from doing it. The strange thing is that, if someone were to hand you a poker which simply looks red-hot — it may just be painted — the unconscious mind will still protect you by not allowing you to grasp the poker.*

"*The same scenario arises whereby if someone is trying to attack me, and in the process of them attacking me I strike them, or attack them in such a way that their unconscious mind expects a strike, then the natural response is to stop and try to protect yourself. In so doing, it's likely they would have difficulty in maintaining balance in such a situation, and as a result you could fall down. On the other hand, if you simply ignore the threat, you can't be knocked down*

Master Harada playing a policeman with Luke, Ziggy Boban's son, in 1989.

without being touched. But if you ignore the threat, then there is no reason why you can't be struck. There is a balance here between having the sensitivity to protect yourself, or ignoring what's actually taking place. Harada Sensei's skill in this area is, in my opinion, to be able to attack the unconscious protection mechanism, so that it believes there is a threat."

Readers will note, therefore, that instructors may be only able to demonstrate such a technique on students who have been so conditioned/self-conditioned. Master Tesshu is reported to have performed his projection feats on his own students, as did Master Ueshiba. (Remember that Egami studied Aikido, and it is a strong possibility that he may have set-up a mental expectation, of which he could have been consciously quite unaware, as to what an encounter with Ueshiba would produce). Ziggy Boban tells of an interesting little incident that occurred at the 1974 Summer School at Keele University. *"During the* (midnight) *session, Sensei engaged in kumite with a bokuto against George Watts, another senior grade. When discussing the practice later, George said that Sensei's weapon was as if it were telescopic, and as he* (George) *tried to advance, the bokuto pushed him in his forehead ... though, in fact, there was no contact. However, Sensei felt somewhat disappointed, saying he had been concentrating too much."* Master Harada is, of course, aware of all the complications surrounding practising with his own students but has taken the leap forward and professed the belief that it should be possible to extend this phenomena to all opponents at all times. Certainly, Marie Kellett notes that there is a great deal of difference between Master Harada's disorientation of a student when compared to other senior grades. *"I can speak from my own experience and other seniors who have seen and experienced both* [types of technique] *and they are worlds apart..."*

Master Harada has made Karate his way of life. He lives Karate and will no doubt die practising Karate — and this is how it should be. If anyone can detect this elusive 'special' power, if indeed it exists, Harada must be up there — at least if experience, intellect and effort are part of the equation. It is hoped that he may find what he has spent the last 40 years searching for. As Marie Kellett put it: *"He sets himself very high standards...and expects his students, especially the senior grades, to follow that example. But because of his sincerity as a person it is not difficult to follow him in that pursuit...He believes that it's important we can show aspects of his Karate and prove physically, explain it logically. If we cannot do this, then people will say only Sensei Harada could do this or he was special. If this happens all his life's work will finish with his passing. But, of course, as an individual and what he has achieved, he is very special to us."* Whilst the spirit and essence of Master Harada, his Karate, will live on in his students, he explains that there is no obligation to the next generation. *"Karate is a challenge to my life, my life...I am running a marathon,"* he said, *"I do not pass the baton".*

"The impact of meeting and training with Sensei Harada has changed my whole life," wrote Marie, and she no doubt echoes the thought of many students in many countries around the globe. Marie knows, perhaps above most of us, that a true Karate master should not be judged solely on his influence and behaviour in the training hall. Isn't the planet Earth a dojo, after all? *"His teachings have influenced my life in many ways,"* commented Steve Hope. And Ken Waight wrote, 23 years after his last practice with the master: *"He opened up a way for me and brought a deep*

"If the quality of a person's life is changed for the better through the practice of Karate, and they are able to share these benefits with their family and others, I am pleased"
— Mitsusuke Harada . . . Karate Master.

resilience and power of purpose into my life which has helped me through many difficult times… I'm sure that, along with many others, he has been a diamond through which we have seen the refined light of Karate in its breadth and depth."

To be an educator, simply by one's normal day-to-day manners and view of life, is so very rare and far more important than mere technique or the acquisition of power. Master Harada shares this characteristic with his famous teachers. When the author asked the master what gave him the greatest pleasure about the development of his students, he did not answer that their kata should be good, or their punches must be strong, or that their kicks must be fast. No, he simply replied: *"If the quality of a person's life is changed for the better through the practice of Karate, and they are able to share these benefits with their family and others, I am pleased."* What is important is how much Karate means to the individual. It is about emotional investment — it is about being human. Tony Lima expressed the sentiment nicely in a heart-felt passage: *"Outside the dojo Sensei has been a kind and good friend to me. He never once forgets to send me a Christmas card or birthday cards to my two daughters. He has advised and guided me…fate has been kind…It is an honour to be a friend and pupil of Sensei, and I shall treasure the relationship 'til the end of my days."*

Well, all things must come to an end, and the wild dove's coo is beginning to fade in my ears. The gods have been patient, and I must not overstay my welcome.

Mitsusuke Harada is a special person. He wasn't born special, but became so as a result of dedication to the ideals and practice of a hard and demanding art. He has become rich, not in money, but in warmth and understanding. In his generosity, he has been prepared to freely share this wisdom, and in so doing, has positively affected the lives of many people — the mark of true achievement. It has to be said now, then, before the spirit of Hermes finally departs, becomes another dream, that of all the many senior teachers of Karate the author has known, none appears to have touched their pupils so deeply, nor is more dearly loved, than Harada Sensei. And, at the end of the day, a man so loved can truly sleep well, for he may rest in the knowledge that his work really was well done.

The Author

Clive Layton began his martial arts training with Judo in 1960. Studying sculpture and design at art school before becoming a teacher, it was during the early Seventies that he began Shotokan Karate under the guidance of Hirokazu Kanazawa. A strong believer in the philosophy of combined mind and body development in the pursuit of excellence, he read for both masters and doctorate degrees in psychology from the University of London to compliment his daily physical training.

Doctor Layton, who is a Chartered Psychologist, has published many learned scientific papers in the fields of personality, stress and mental health. He has also worked on radio and television in connection with his research work. In addition, Dr. Layton has written numerous articles for various magazines on both the technical and psychological aspects of Karate, has co-authored research notes with Masters Morio Higaonna and Steve Arneil, and is the author of five much-acclaimed books: *'Conversations With Karate Masters', 'Unmasking The Martial Artist', 'Mysteries Of The Martial Arts', 'Mind Training For The Martial Arts'*, and *'Training With Funakoshi'*. A respected, traditional Karate-ka, who lives and trains far from the madding crowd, he currently holds the rank of 5th Dan.

Photo Credits

Mitsusuke Harada: pages 2, 4, 6, 7, 9, 22, 23, 25, 36, 39, 40, 41, 45, 47, 48, 53, 54, 57, 59, 65, 67, 69, 71, 72, 73, 77, 83, 86, 90, 91, 92, 93, 96, 99, 101, 103, 104, 105, 106, 107, 109, 110, 112, 125 PLUS photographs reproduced by kind courtesy of the publishers of the following Japanese language titles: pages 10/11, 16, 19, 28, 33 '*50 Years Of The Shotokan*' (published in 1988 by the Shotokai); page 15 '*Karate Nyumon*' by Genshin Hironishi (published in 1955); pages 21, 63 '*Hiryu: 50 Years Of Chuo University Karate Club*' (published by Chuo University); pages 42, 43 '*60 Years Of Waseda Karate Club*' (published by Waseda University); page 61 '*Memories Of The Late Shigeru Egami*' (published in 1981 by the Shotokai); page 147 '*Karate-Do*' by Shigeru Egami (published in 1970); page 51 '*Karate-Do*' (published in 1977 by Sozo Company).

Professor Bernard Mathieu: pages 13, 94, 137, 152, 171, 173, 175, 177, 179, 181. 187, 189, 190, 191, 199.

André Louka *('Dojo Arts Martiaux'* France*):* front cover and pages 159, 161, 163, 168.

Sylvio Dokov: facing title page and pages 159, 161, 163, 168.

Ken Waight: pages 123, 135, 139, 145.

Zygmunt Boban: pages 123, 135, 139, 145.

Stanley Pranin (*'Aikido Journal'* Japan): pages 75, 79, 80.

Hampshire Chronicle Group Newspapers: pages 143, 148/149.

Henri D. Plee: pages 117, 121.

William Haggerty: pages 156, 185.

Patrick McCarthy: pages 12, 31.

Clive Layton: page 155. **Masatoshi Nakayama:** page 27. **Richard Kim:** page 55. **Franco Chen:** page 81. **Arthur Tansley:** page 84. **Kodansha International Ltd:** page 89 (from '*Karate-Do Kyohan: The Master Text*' by Gichin Funakoshi). **Terry O'Neill:** page 89. **Steve Bellamy:** page 97. **D. J. Gossling:** page 115 (supplied by Mr. Vernon Bell). **Brian Hammond:** page 116. **Shaun Slater:** page 119. **Taiji Kase:** page 127. **Ronnie Watt:** page 128. **Robin O'Tani:** page 130. **Tony Lima/Steve Hope:** page 165. **John Sheppard:** page 183. **Southern Newspapers PLC Southampton:** page 201. **Rachel Layton:** page 207.

Useful Addresses

KARATE·DO

SHOTOKAI

Prinicipal
Mitsusuke Harada

For All General Enquiries contact:
Karate-Do Shotokai Administrator
Jonathan de'Claire BSc.(Hons)
36 Laburnam Way, Penarth,
Vale of Glamorgan,
United Kingdom,CF64 3NF.

Correspondence to Master Harada:
KDS, 20 Shakespeare Road,
Cwmbran,Gwent,NP44 4LW, G.B.

Durham University Shotokai Karate Club
have a Web page that offers information
and KDS contact numbers.The Address is
http://w.w.w.dur.ac.uk/Shotokai.

Shihan
Tsutomu Ohshima

Shotokan Karate Of America National Headquarters

2500 S. La Cienega Boulevard,
Los Angeles,
California 90034, USA.

Ordering This Book

Further copies of *'Karate Master - The Life And Times Of Mitsusuke Harada'* can be obtained directly from:
Bushido Publications, PO Box 15, Liverpool,
Merseyside L19 7PE, England.
Tel: (+44) 151 494 1176. Fax: (+44) 151 494 1192.
Trade Enquiries Welcomed
(Wholesalers, Retailers, Dojo Secretaries etc.)
Excellent Discounts For Quantity Sales.

USA Distribution/Sales

Dragon Associates Inc. PO Box 6039, Thousand Oaks,
California 91359.
Tel +1(805)371 6222. Fax +1(805)371 6224.

Forthcoming Books from.

The Twelve Kata required for Advancement from Beginner through to Black Belt

KIHON KATA
HEIAN SHODAN
HEIAN NIDAN
HEIAN SANDAN
HEIAN YONDAN
HEIAN GODAN
TEKKI SHODAN
BASSAI DAI
KANKU DAI
JION
ENPI
HANGETSU

SHOTOKAN KARATE
KATA
FROM BEGINNER TO BLACK BELT

By TERRY O'NEILL
Illustrated by CHRIS EVANS

A senior British Karate-ka who was Seven times National Kata Champion and a professional Artist/Karate-ka have combined their skills to produce an outstanding textbook on the first twelve Shotokan Kata. Several years in production, this book captures in a unique way the dynamic essence and precise step-by-step movements of the kata skills necessary for advancement to *Shodan* (1st Degree Black Belt) level.

Variations in technique are shown along with practical applications of selected kata movements.

... Bushido Publications

NEW EDITIONS of these popular titles by Dr. Clive Layton

'UNMASKING THE MARTIAL ARTIST'

Self discovery is one of the central aims of Japanese Budo and *'Unmasking...'*
seeks to help students acheive this by becoming more introspective...Why do
people practice Martial Arts? Is it some deep-rooted inferiority complex? or is
physical body-type a causative factor? Maybe they are drawn by a death
instinct; Is it a high need for acheivement? or a fear of failure? Does it all come
down to sex in the end? How fast are the punches of low grade Karate-ka compared to Black-Belts up to 5th Dan? What sort of personality do Masters pos-
sess? The answers to these and many more questions are to be found within this
unique book... and there are some surprises!

'TRAINING WITH FUNAKOSHI'

A delightful book about the famous Okinawan Karate Master, **Gichin
Funakoshi.** Around the facts, Dr.Layton weaves a simple and unobtrusive story,
focussing on the period from 1922, just after the Master's famous demonstration in Tokyo, to his death in 1957. Funakoshi's efforts to establish the art on
mainland Japan; the 'Golden Era of Training' in the Twenties and Thirties; the
war years and the difficulties thereafter, are all investigated.
Not only a valuable reference work brimming with information, *'Training
With...'* also gently touches the very essence of the *'Way of Shoto'* itself.

'MIND TRAINING FOR THE MARTIAL ARTS'

Arguably Dr. Layton's most popular work to date— the first printing quickly
sold out— *'Mind Training...'* is an outstanding how-to-do-it text. An easy-to-fol-
low approach guides readers through 38 mind-training exercises specially
designed to complement Martial Arts practise. The chapters focus on the importance of relaxation and concentration, and how to obtain them; the skills
involved in mental imagery and planning, and so on.
One of those rare books of benefit to beginners and advanced grades alike.

'MYSTERIES OF THE MARTIAL ARTS'

Bringing to light some of the phenomena associated with the Martial Arts and
the people who practise them, this absorbing book is packed full of unusual
material and makes fascinating reading.
For example: The concept of *Ki*, or intrinsic energy, is examined; the existence of
a sixth-sense is highlighted, and some extraordinary scientific findings made
clear... Similarly, *Kime*, or focussed energy, is investigated and the World famous
Karate Master **Hirokazu Kanazawa,** talks about his amazing ability to selectively
break boards in a stack.

Recommended Further Reading ....

"*The finest English language martial arts magazine available.*"
Master Morio Higaonna, Okinawan Goju-Ryu Karate.

" *Finally, a magazine for the forgotten, serious martial artist.*"
Stanley Pranin, Editor-in-Chief, 'Aiki Journal'.

" *I recommend FAI for a truly international view of the martial arts.*"
Shihan Takayuki Kubota, International Karate Association.

Terry O'Neill's FIGHTING ARTS INTERNATIONAL

Founded in 1972 and published 6 times a year, *FAI* is available
from selective retail outlets, *or* on direct subscription - along
with a range of '*Collectors Early Editions*' - from
Bushido Publications, P.O. Box 15, Liverpool, Merseyside
L19 7PE, England.
Tel: (+44)151 494 1176. Fax: (+44)151 494 1192.

USA Distribution/Sales

Dragon Associates Inc. PO Box 6039, Thousand Oaks,
California 91359.
Tel +1(805)371 6222. Fax +1(805)371 6224.